This book belongs to:

....

Project Editor Clare Lloyd
Senior Art Editor Rachael Parfitt Hunt
Edited by Abi Luscombe
Text by Ben Hubbard, Andrea Mills, Graeme Williams
Subject Consultant Helen Scales
Designed by Karen Hood, Hannah Moore,
Rhys Thomas, Sadie Thomas
Additional Illustrations Kitty Glavin
Project Picture Researcher Sakshi Saluja
Production Editor Dragana Puvacic
Production Controller John Casey
Jacket Designer Elle Ward
Jacket Co-ordinator Issy Walsh
Managing Editor Penny Smith
Deputy Art Director Mabel Chan
Publishing Director Sarah Larter

First published in Great Britain in 2021 by
Dorling Kindersley Limited
DK, One Embassy Gardens, 8 Viaduct Gardens,
London, SW11 7BW

The authorised representative in the EEA is
Dorling Kindersley Verlag GmbH. Arnulfstr. 124,
80636 Munich, Germany

Copyright © 2021 Dorling Kindersley Limited
A Penguin Random House Company
10 9 8 7 6 5 4 3 2 1
001–322997–Sep/2021

A CIP catalogue record for this book
is available from the British Library.
ISBN: 978-0-2414-8577-4

Printed and bound in China

For the curious
www.dk.com

MIX
Paper from
responsible sources
FSC™ C018179

This book was made with Forest
Stewardship Council™ certified
paper—one small step in DK's
commitment to a sustainable
future. For more information go to
www.dk.com/our-green-pledge

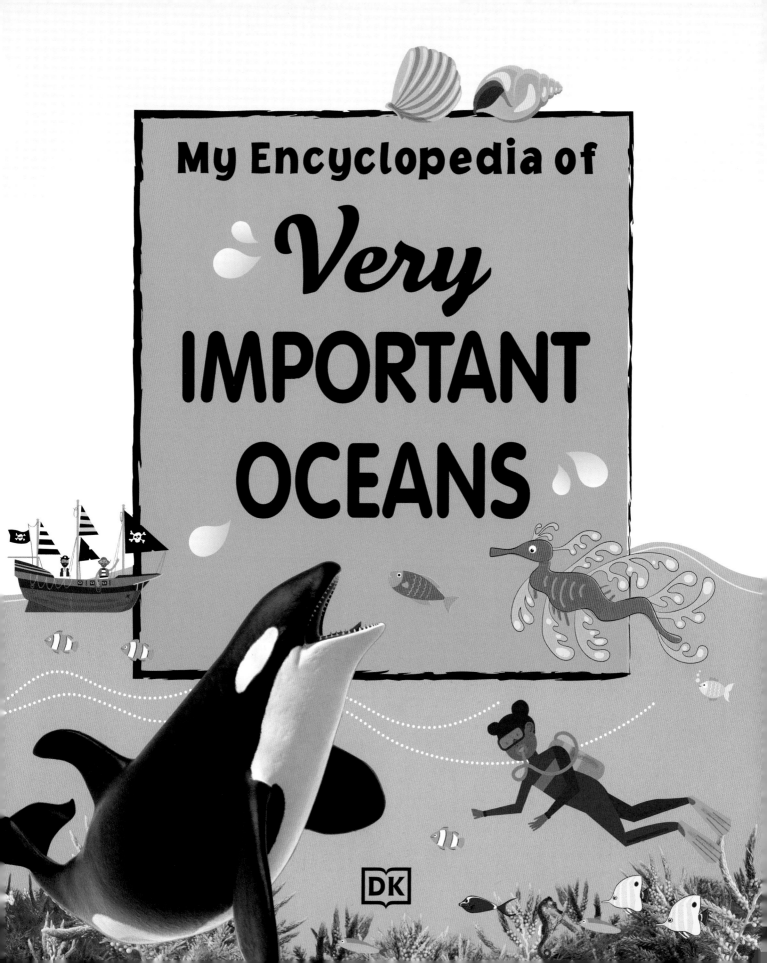

My Encyclopedia of
Very
IMPORTANT
OCEANS

DK

Contents

Ocean environments

Oceans and us

Earth's

oceans

Take the plunge and go on a wet and wild trip around **our watery world**. Dive into salty seas, navigate wacky waves and weird weather, and travel deep down to the ocean floor — you'll have a whale of a time!

Blue planet

Welcome to our watery world! Oceans cover huge areas of our planet. They are the **biggest sources** of water on Earth and are home to lots of wildlife.

Water and land

There is more water than land on Earth. Water takes up more than **two-thirds** of the entire surface! The rest of Earth's surface is home to the seven continents and thousands of islands.

We still don't know all the animals that live in the ocean.

I'm the largest creature in the ocean.

Shrimp

Blue whale

Clouds

True blue

The oceans look **blue** because of **sunlight**. The Sun's rays contain all the colours of the rainbow. When bright sunlight shines on the oceans, the water takes in all of the colours except for blue. The blue rays then reflect off the water for us to see.

There's so much water on Earth!

Ocean

Land

The ocean formed over FOUR BILLION years ago!

The oceans

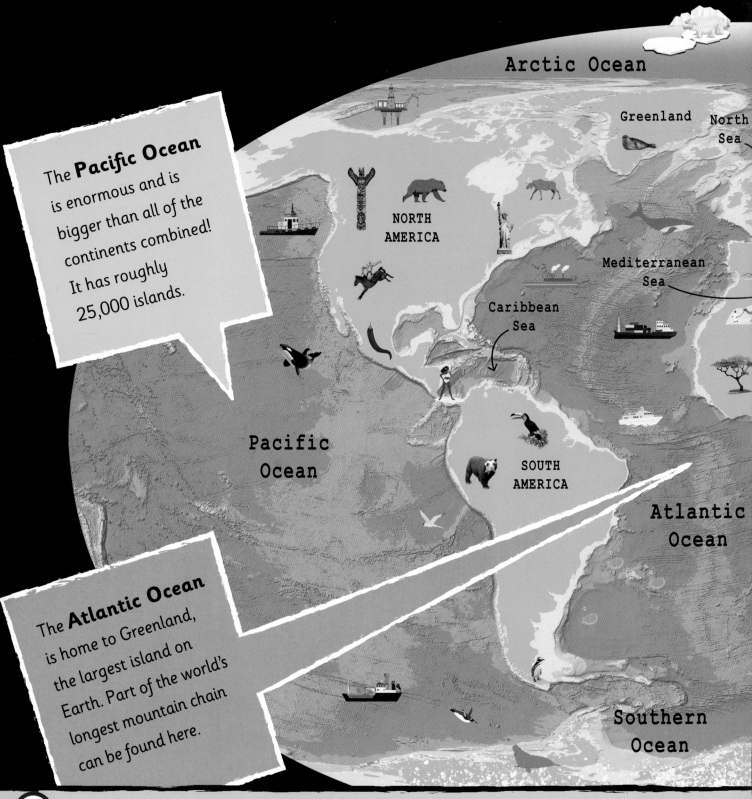

Arctic Ocean

Greenland

North Sea

The Pacific Ocean is enormous and is bigger than all of the continents combined! It has roughly 25,000 islands.

NORTH AMERICA

Mediterranean Sea

Caribbean Sea

Pacific Ocean

SOUTH AMERICA

Atlantic Ocean

The Atlantic Ocean is home to Greenland, the largest island on Earth. Part of the world's longest mountain chain can be found here.

Southern Ocean

The Pacific Ocean contains **MORE** water than **ALL**

The **Arctic Ocean** is the smallest of the five oceans.

Earth has **FIVE OCEANS** that are connected to form one huge body of water. Smaller areas of the oceans are called **SEAS**.

The **Indian Ocean** is the warmest ocean in the world, which makes it difficult for some wildlife to live there.

Baltic Sea

Black Sea

EUROPE

ASIA

Adriatic Sea

Persian Gulf

Red Sea

Arabian Sea

AFRICA

Indian Ocean

AUSTRALIA

97 per cent of Earth's water is in the oceans.

ANTARCTICA

Icebergs are found in the **Southern Ocean** during all seasons. It has the coldest waters of all the oceans.

the other oceans put together!

Oceans apart

What's special about Earth's **five oceans**?

Let's dive in and find out!

The first ocean formed billions of years ago.

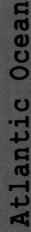

Easter Island is a famous island in the Pacific. It is known for its huge, stone statues, called "Moai".

Galápagos Islands

The marine iguana lives on the Galápagos Islands, in the Pacific Ocean.

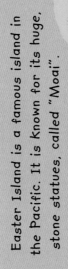

Easter Island

Pacific Ocean

Earth's **biggest** and **deepest** ocean is home to thousands of islands. Nearly half of all ocean water is in the Pacific Ocean.

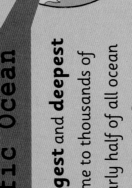

Atlantic Ocean

The Atlantic Ocean separates North and South America from Europe and Africa. It is the **second largest** ocean, and has a mix of warm and cold waters.

Namibia

Tropical storms, called "hurricanes", often form over the Atlantic.

The southern king crab lives in cold Atlantic waters.

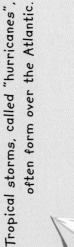

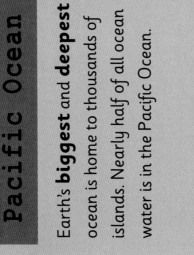

Cold air from the Atlantic meets dry air from the Namib Desert, causing thick fogs in Namibia. Many ships have run aground there.

Arctic Ocean

Baffin Bay

The Arctic is the **coldest** ocean. In the winter, it is mostly covered in a thick layer of ice.

Icebergs from Baffin Bay, in the Arctic, drift south into the North Atlantic, where they are a danger to ships.

Ringed seals live and hunt in Arctic waters.

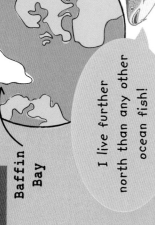

I live further north than any other ocean fish!

Arctic cod

Indian Ocean

The Indian Ocean is south of Asia and lies between Africa and Australia. It's the **warmest** of the five oceans.

Maldives

I feast on seagrass in warm coastal waters.

Dugong

The Maldives is made up of more than 1,000 coral islands. They are popular with scuba divers.

Undersea earthquakes in the Indian Ocean lead to huge, destructive waves called "tsunamis".

Southern Ocean

The cold Southern Ocean surrounds Antarctica and is the only ocean that goes all the way **around the globe.**

Antarctica

I'm the largest seabird in the world!

The wandering albatross flies huge distances over the Southern Ocean.

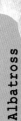

Albatross

Most of Earth's icebergs are found in Antarctic waters.

Salty seas

Salt from the **rocks** and **soil** on land washes into rivers and travels into the sea, making it salty.

Salt water

We can't see the salt in the water because it has dissolved. But, if the sea water **evaporates** (turns into gas), the grains of salt would be left behind.

It's easy to float on salt water in the Dead Sea.

The Dead Sea is a salt lake between Israel and Jordan. The water there is ten times saltier than sea water!

Salt is the simple name for the mineral sodium chloride.

If **ALL** the water from the oceans was evaporated, the leftover salt would form a layer on land that is as high as a **35-STOREY** building!

Salt water is too salty for me to drink!

Fresh water

Fresh water contains very little salt. Most of Earth's fresh water can be found in **glaciers** and **ice caps**, but it can also be found in rivers.

Only a tiny amount of Earth's water is fresh water.

Ice caps

Fresh water glacier

Sea

River water starts off fresh and picks up salt as it travels towards the sea.

An estuary is where river water mixes with salty sea water.

Most of the water on Earth is salt water.

The saltiness of water is called "salinity".

Fish can drink sea water. Our gills get rid of the extra salt.

Sea water runs through a starfish's body instead of blood.

1

Heat from the Sun evaporates sea water. This means water changes from a liquid to a gas, and rises.

The water cycle

Imagine going **up** and **down** a slide forever — climbing up, sliding down, running around, and climbing back up again! This is like the world's water cycle.

How does it work?

The Earth always has the same amount of water, but it is **constantly moving** around. Water builds up in the sky, falls on the ground, travels down to the ocean, and heads up to the sky again.

Gas

Water CHANGES STATE in the water cycle. It can be a solid, a liquid, or a gas.

5

The Sun heats up the water again, and the cycle repeats itself.

Solid

Liquid

2

The gas, called water vapour, cools and makes tiny water droplets, which form clouds.

3

Clouds produce rain, snow, or hail, which is called precipitation.

What is weather?

The weather describes what is happening in the air around us. The weather forecast predicts what the weather will be like. It can be hot, cold, sunny, wet, windy, stormy, or snowy.

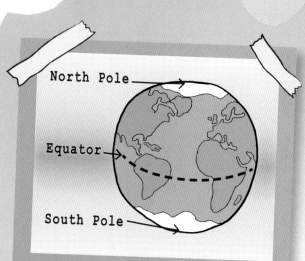

North Pole

Equator

South Pole

Weather that is typical to an area is called a climate. For example, the climate is hot around the equator, but cold around the North and South Poles.

The weather report

4

Water falls on land, collects in streams and rivers, and is carried back to the ocean.

Ancient oceans

The ocean formed **billions** of years ago, followed by Earth's first ocean animals.

Ancient ocean creatures

The first ocean creatures were **marine invertebrates** (animals without a backbone) with hard shells. Later, **vertebrates** (animals with a backbone), including marine reptiles and mammals, roamed the seas.

500 million years ago
the first marine invertebrates filled the seas.

250 million years ago
enormous reptiles lived in the oceans.

Trilobites lived long before the dinosaurs.

Ichthyosaur means "fish lizard" in Greek.

For millions of years, the ocean was teeming with trilobites. They crawled along the seabed or swam through the water. Trilobites had hard bodies and looked a bit like woodlice.

The ichthyosaur lived when dinosaurs roamed the Earth. It looked a bit like a dolphin, and had a long, pointy snout.

The first ocean

When the ocean formed, Earth had **no continents**. Then, volcanoes created rocks and the continents were formed. The water flowed around these continents, and created the different oceans that we know today.

Trilobite fossils are found in ancient rocks.

20 million years ago

Megalodons entered the oceans.

Megalodon is the largest shark in history!

Sharks lived in the oceans long before the Megalodon. It is related to the mako shark and died out more than 1.5 million years ago.

Fossils

Fossils are the rare **remains** of ancient creatures that have been preserved over millions of years.

1

A dead animal is covered in mud and sand.

2

The animal rots, but usually the skeleton and teeth remain and turn to stone.

3

Many years later, the skeleton has dissolved and a fossil is left behind.

Paleontologists study fossils to find out what life was like millions of years ago.

The ocean floor

The bottom of the ocean is a lot like the **land** on Earth. It has mountains, volcanoes, trenches, and a variety of plants and animals.

Continental slope

A slope that joins the continental shelf and the abyssal plain.

Continental shelf

The shallow part of the ocean floor that meets the land.

A coral reef is an area of coral. The top of the reef is usually just above or just below sea level.

Coral reefs cover less than one per cent of the ocean floor.

Abyssal plain

The flat area that covers most of the ocean floor.

Trench

A long, deep channel on the ocean floor.

We live in the Mariana Trench.

Dumbo octopuses

The **deepest ocean trench** is the Mariana Trench. It is 11,034 m (36,200 ft) deep.

Hydrothermal vents are found near volcanoes.

A hydrothermal vent is a hot spring that flows from the seabed. They're hot!

Volcanic island

A volcano with its top above sea level.

Volcano

Volcano

An opening in the seabed where lava and ash erupt into the water.

Ridge

An underwater mountain range that forms when tectonic plates move away from each other.

Seamount

An underwater volcano. Its top is below sea level.

Seamount

The **tallest mountain** in the ocean is Mauna Kea. It's 9,750 m (32,000 ft) tall.

The **deepest diving animal** is the cuvier's beaked whale. It can dive to 3,000 m (nearly 10,000 ft).

The **deepest free dive** in history is 253.2 m (830 ft).

Incredible islands

You might picture an island as a sun-soaked, sandy beach with palm trees, but islands are all quite different. An island is any piece of land entirely **surrounded by water**.

Greenland

Maldives

Big or small

The world's largest island is **Greenland**, which is icy and in the north Atlantic Ocean. There are also lots of tiny islands on Earth called **islets**.

Sandy or stony

The **Maldives** consist of about 1,200 sandy islands. The 21 **Galápagos Islands** are rocky and make a great home for wildlife, such as the giant tortoise.

Island hotspots

Eruptions from inside Earth can split through the ocean floor and create hotspots. Repeated eruptions can form **volcanic islands**, such as the Hawaiian Islands in the Pacific Ocean.

A group of islands is called an "archipelago".

Kilauea in Hawaii is the most active volcano on Earth. It has been erupting non-stop since 1983!

Aleutian Islands

Cyclades

Hot or cold
The **Aleutian Islands** have a cold climate with heavy rain and thick fog, whereas the **Cook Islands** have a tropical climate and sunshine all year round.

Near or far
Tristan da Cunha are a group of islands that is miles from anything else. Other islands, including the **Cyclades** in the Aegean Sea, lie very close to mainland Greece.

I'm a surfer. I catch waves and ride them back to the shore.

Waves

It's fun to jump over waves as they crash onto the shore. But where do waves **come from**, and why do they break?

Wind →

How waves work

When the wind blows across the surface of the ocean, it **whips up waves**. Waves form as water moves in a circular motion. The biggest waves are made by strong, long-lasting winds.

Water moves in a circular motion.

As they grow, waves form different patterns known as **ripples**, **chop**, and **swell**.

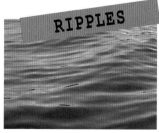

RIPPLES

The wind blows over the surface and small ripples are formed.

CHOP

As the wind keeps blowing, ripples turn into chop.

SWELL

Over time, chop turns into regular waves, called swell.

Surfing curlers

The best waves for surfing are those that curl over to form a **tube**. The "Pipeline" in Oahu, Hawaii, does this, and waves can reach a height of 6 m (20 ft) – that's as tall as a giraffe!

The "Pipeline" in Oahu, Hawaii.

Wave

Very **BIG** waves can cause damage when they hit the shore.

Breaking wave

How big breaking waves form

1 When a wave approaches the shore, the bottom of it hits the shallow seafloor.

2 The circular motion is interrupted, making the wave slower and taller.

3 The water at the top of the wave thins out.

4 The wave curls over and becomes a breaking wave.

Seafloor near the shore

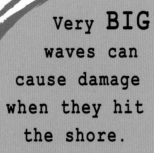

Big, powerful waves can erode (wear down) cliffs, remove sand from beaches, and even knock down walls!

The most powerful waves are caused by earthquakes on the seafloor. These huge waves get bigger as they head towards land.

Currents

Currents are like underwater rivers that push ocean water around the world. There are **surface** and **deepwater** currents in the ocean.

Global Conveyor Belt

The Global Conveyor Belt is one of the longest currents in the world. It moves cold water and hot surface water around the world in a slow, **1,000-year journey**.

Slow-moving, circular currents cause trash to gather and spin.

Greenland

1

North America

Atlantic Ocean

South America

Pacific Ocean

Southern Ocean

2

1 Cold, salty water at the poles sinks and moves slowly south.

2 The deepwater current mixes with the cold waters of Antarctica.

Water CONSTANTLY FLOWS between the five oceans.

Arctic Ocean

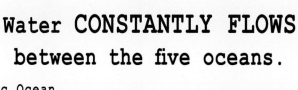

In 1992, a cargo ship spilled thousands of rubber ducks into the ocean. Currents sent the ducks all over the world!

Northern Europe would be much colder without warm currents flowing from the Gulf Stream.

Europe

4

Asia

Africa

Currents move heat from the warm tropics to cold polar waters.

Indian Ocean

Warm current

Pacific Ocean

Australia

There may be 2,000 more of us still floating in the ocean!

3

Cold current

Antarctica

3 Some water flows into the Indian and Pacific oceans, where it rises into a warm surface current.

4 The surface current travels towards Greenland, where it gets colder and completes the cycle.

Tides

Every day, the level of the ocean on the coast rises and falls. These are called "tides" and are caused by the **Moon's gravity**, which is an invisible force that pulls on the Earth.

High or low?

When the Moon's gravity pulls ocean water towards it, the sea level rises. This is **high tide**. When the sea level falls, this is called **low tide**.

Low tide

When the Moon's pull is weak, the water levels fall. The waves don't reach far up the beach.

LOW TIDE:
the sea goes out

Hide tide

When the Moon's pull is strong, the water levels rise. The waves reach high up the beach.

HIGH TIDE:
the sea comes in

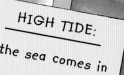

Most coasts have **TWO HIGH TIDES** and **TWO LOW**

The Earth takes a day to do a full turn.

Turning tides

Planet Earth rotates as the Moon travels around it. Tides rise or fall depending on which parts of the Earth's oceans are **facing** the Moon.

EARTH'S TIDES

The Moon orbits the Earth

The Moon's gravitational pull

EARTH

High tide

Low tide

High tide

MOON

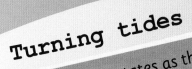

! WARNING
Water can quickly cover the beach so it's important to know when tides are coming in and out.

High tides occur on both sides of the Earth at the same time.

Rock-pooling!

At low tide, you might find tiny creatures, such as crabs, in rock pools.

TIDES   each day.

Coastal erosion

Even the most gentle ocean waves are very powerful. Over hundreds of years, they rub away rock, wearing it down into **smaller** and **smoother** pieces. This is called **erosion**.

Rocks fall off the cliff.

Waves erode the bottom of the cliff.

1 Waves crash into the bottom of cliffs. Over time, they wear down the rock.

2 Eventually, the bottom is so worn down that it can't hold the heavy cliff above, and it crumbles into the sea.

Break it down!

Over time, rocks are **broken** into **tiny pieces**. Powerful waves and colliding rocks mean huge boulders eventually become tiny grains of sand.

Boulders

Pebbles

Hard rocks, such as granite, erode slowly.

Soft rocks, such as chalk, break down quickly.

Where land sticks out into the ocean, waves can grind it to form a "sea cave". If the waves break through the cave, a "sea arch" is formed.

3 The waves pick up the rocky material, but they can't hold onto it all.

4 The heaviest rocks and pebbles fall at the top of the beach, while tiny grains of sand are left by the shore.

The Yonaguni Monument

Japan has its own unique rock formations — giant, flat, **underwater "steps"** carved into the rock. Scientists can't decide if these were made naturally or by people.

Shingle

Sand

Danger zone

Most of us check the weather reports before going outside. But the threat of rain is nothing compared to the **natural hazards** affecting Earth's oceans. You are now entering the danger zone!

Floods
Heavy rainfall can cause floods, but so can rising sea levels. If the water gets too high, it can flood the coastline and destroy buildings.

When a hurricane reaches land it can destroy cars, trees, and buildings.

Hurricanes
Tropical storms, called "hurricanes", are formed over the North Atlantic and the Northeast Pacific Ocean. They can be as wide as a city and last for days at a time.

Hurricanes and cyclones are both tropical storms but are given different names depending on where they appe-

Cyclones
Strong, **spiralling winds** can form quickl in hot temperatures ove the South Pacific and Indian Ocean. Cyclones travel at breathtaking speeds.

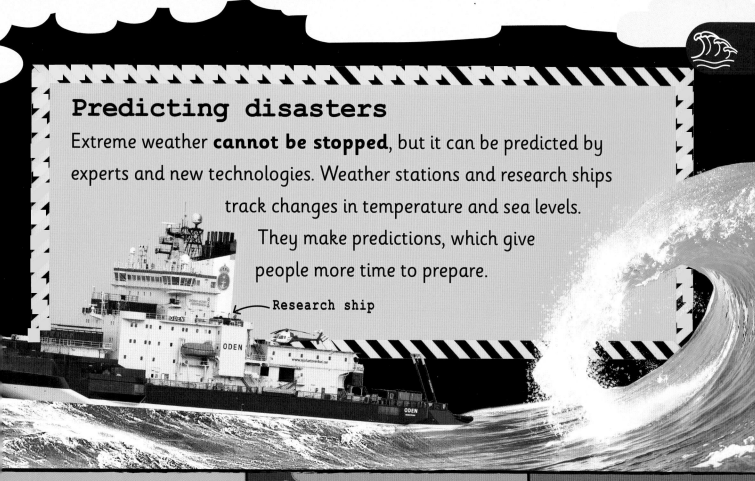

Predicting disasters

Extreme weather **cannot be stopped**, but it can be predicted by experts and new technologies. Weather stations and research ships track changes in temperature and sea levels. They make predictions, which give people more time to prepare.

Research ship

Whirlpools

If two currents meet in the ocean, they form a **swirling** area of water called a "whirlpool". The strongest whirlpools have the power to drag swimmers and boats under the water.

Volcanic eruptions

Most volcanic activity takes place underwater. Volcanoes erupt in **hot spots**, throwing out lava and ash. Ocean water cools the lava and ash down, turning it into solid rock.

Tsunamis

Shockwaves caused by volcanoes and earthquakes can produce dangerous **walls of water**, called "tsunamis". They move quickly towards the coastline and when they reach land, they destroy everything in their path.

Meet the

animals

Some of the weirdest and most wonderful creatures on Earth **inhabit the oceans**. Our waters are home to a variety of creatures, from small sea dragons to whopper whales. Dive in to meet the locals – but watch out for sneaky sea snakes!

Small wonders

Good things come in small packages! These tiny creatures are **critical** to the way the ocean works.

Zooplankton

Zooplankton are **microscopic** marine creatures that drift in the ocean and eat tiny, plant-like phytoplankton. Larger animals depend on them for their survival.

zooplankton

Krill

This shrimp-like zooplankton is eaten by whales, squid, penguins, and fish. Huge swarms of krill have even been seen from **space**!

The total weight of krill in the ocean is more than the total weight of all the people in the world!

Copepod

This little creature is a type of zooplankton and is the most common animal in the ocean! It has long **antennae** to find food, and keeps the ocean clean by eating algae, bacteria, and dead organisms.

Antennae

The word "PLANKTON" comes from the Greek word for "DRIFTER".

Many plankton are carried along on ocean tides and currents.

Sea gooseberry

Sea gooseberry

Starting life as a jelly-like larvae, as the gooseberry grows, it **develops** big eyes and an even bigger appetite.

Arrow worm

The see-through arrow worm is a fast swimmer. It uses **hooks** on its head to catch prey, such as copepods.

Arrow worm

Spectacular sponges

I wear a sponge to protect my nose when I forage for food.

Sponges don't have a head or heart – they can't even move! These **simple animals** belong to a group of sea creatures without a backbone, called "marine invertebrates".

Stove-pipe sponge

Don't touch the red one, it will hurt!

Fire sponge

Stove-pipe sponges have pink and purple tubes. They live in deep water, where strong currents cannot break off their fragile tubes.

Fire sponges are covered with a chemical that causes a burning rash when touched. This stops most predators from eating them.

Sponge fossil

Sponges are some of the oldest
living things on Earth.

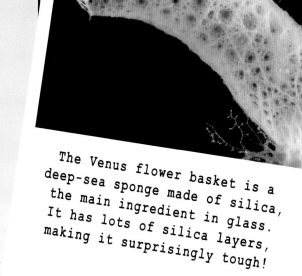

The Venus flower basket is a
deep-sea sponge made of silica,
the main ingredient in glass.
It has lots of silica layers,
making it surprisingly tough!

Sponge survival

Sponges have hard, inner skeletons that
anchor them in place. They are also filled
with **pores** that suck in seawater. Tiny
hairs trap food before the water is pushed
out again.

Aaahhchooo

Orange sponge
encrusted on
a rock.

Watch out,
that one is
poisonous!

Sneezing sponge

The glass rope sponge has
been caught "**sneezing**".
It sucks in water and then
very slowly sneezes it out
again – it can last
for weeks!

Encrusting sponges are flat, brightly coloured
sponges. Many are poisonous, but some predators
have adapted so that they can eat them anyway.

Jazzy jellies

Jellyfish are not actually fish! They don't have a brain, a heart, blood, or bones. Instead, jellyfish have soft bodies, with long, **stinging tentacles** to stun their prey.

Box-shaped body (bell) with a mouth on the bottom.

The box jelly is as small as a grape!

Box jellyfish

Up to fifteen tentacles on each corner of the bell.

Deadly drifter

Beware – the box jellyfish is deadly! One touch from its tentacles can kill a person. It has over **5,000 stinging cells** on its tentacles, which contain deadly venom.

Eeeek! I'm out of here!

A group of jellyfish is called a BLOOM or SWARM.

Lion's mane jellyfish

Moon jellyfish

The lion's mane jellyfish is the world's biggest jellyfish. It uses its **shaggy tentacles** like a net to catch prey.

Moon jellyfish have **translucent bells** – this means you can see straight through them. Jellyfish bodies are made mostly of water, so if they wash up on land they collapse.

Jellyfish come in lots of shapes and colours.

Golden jellyfish

Flower hat jelly

Cannonball jellyfish

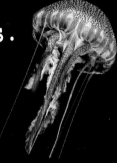
Mauve stinger jellyfish

Jellyfish do not have a brain, but respond to messages from their nerves, which sense heat and touch.

Emperor Hirohito of Japan was crazy about jellyfish. He spent Monday and Thursday afternoons studying and writing scientific papers about them.

Shining stars

Starfish have no brain or heart, but they can still move around using their **sticky arms**. These colourful creatures really are the stars of the show!

Common starfish

Blue sea star

Armed and dangerous

Most starfish have five arms, but some have as many as 50! If a starfish loses an arm, it can **regrow** it.

Feet first

The arms of a starfish have hundreds of **tiny tubes** that work like little feet. At the end of each arm is an eye.

Necklace starfish

Red spine star

Some sea stars can REGROW their entire body from just one arm!

Starfish arm

Starfish eye

There are about 2,000

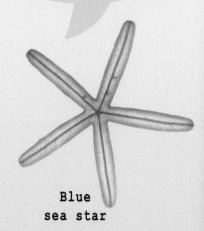

Some of us match the seabed, while others are colourful to scare off attackers.

Red cushion star

Sunflower stars

Sunflower stars are some of the biggest and fastest sea stars.

Inside out

The tubes on a starfish's arms seize food, such as molluscs and corals, and bring them to its mouth. The star **pushes its stomach** out of its body, digests the food, then sucks its stomach back inside!

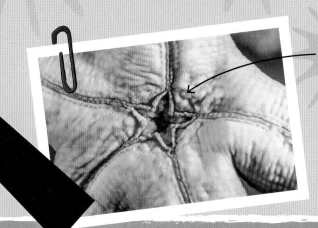

Starfish mouth

We are family

Starfish, sea cucumbers, and sea urchins are all part of the **echinoderm** family. They have spiny skin and tube-like feet, but no backbone, brain, or heart.

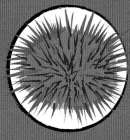

When attacked, **sea cucumbers** shoot out a sticky substance to trap predators.

Sea urchins have sharp spines to prevent enemies from coming too close.

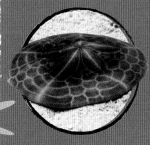

Found on the seabed, **sand dollars** look like squashed sea urchins with smaller spines.

different TYPES of STARFISH.

Spectacular shells

Many animals have hard, outer shells that protect their soft bodies. Some sea creatures **live inside** them, while others wear them like **armour**.

Hermit crab

The hermit crab is not born with a shell. Instead, it **finds** an empty sea-snail shell to move into!

Sea turtle

The sea turtle has a shell that **protects its insides**. Unlike a tortoise, it cannot tuck its head or legs into its shell.

Have you ever held an EMPTY SHELL up to your ear?

Coconut carrier

Soft-bodied octopuses do not have shells, but sometimes they carry a **coconut shell** for protection. When threatened, they climb inside and snap the shell shut!

Cowry shell

COWRY SHELLS were once used as money.

Clam

A clam lives inside **two shells**. It is found on sandy beaches around the world.

Abalone

The abalone is a type of **sea snail**. Its gills release water through holes in its shell.

Chiton

The chiton's eight **shell plates** allow it to roll into a ball of **armour** if it falls from its rock.

Lobster

As it ages, the lobster sheds its hard shell to reveal a shiny new shell that has been growing underneath! This is called **moulting**.

Some say you can hear the OCEAN!

47

Snappy crabs

Finding a crab in a rock pool is a holiday highlight, but there is lots more to these **speedy scuttlers** than meets the eye.

Claw

Leg

Crabs' sharp claws, called "pincers", come in useful for gripping, catching prey, and fighting attackers.

Sideways motion

Instead of getting their eight **jointed legs** tangled up by moving forwards, crabs scuttle **sideways**. This allows them to move easily and quickly across the sand.

This crab's real eyes are here.

Crabs have eyes on stalks, to look out for danger. If they spot a threat, crabs will burrow themselves into the sand.

Mass movement

Every year, **millions** of red crabs on Christmas Island, Australia, travel from the forest to the ocean. This incredible journey takes about a week.

I'm known as a "scavenger of the shoreline" because I'm not fussy about what I eat!

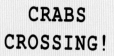

CRABS CROSSING!

Crabs eat shrimp.

Crustaceans

Most crustaceans **live in water**, but a few live on land. They have hard shells, jointed legs, and no backbone. Crabs are the best known crustaceans, but let's meet some others.

Lobsters have pincers for catching food and defending themselves.

Unable to move, **barnacles** stick themselves to rocks and ships.

Mantis shrimp use their hidden, second set of legs to attack prey.

As they drift through the water, tiny **krill** are eaten by lots of marine creatures.

49

Brilliant bivalves

The empty shells found on the seashore were once the homes of soft-bodied creatures called **molluscs**. Those with two shells, joined by a hinge, are known as "bivalves".

Clams

Shell safety

The hard shells of bivalves keep them safe. They create their shells over time using **minerals** in sea water. Some bivalves have a muscular "foot", which sticks out from the shell to help them move around.

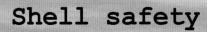

Clam siphon

Clams

Clams have a long tube, called a **siphon**, to **breathe** and filter food from the water.

Pearl

Oysters

The **pearls** that oysters create are made in self-defence. They wrap invaders in a substance called mother-of-pearl to trap them inside their shell.

Mussels

Mussels can stay in the same place for a long time. They **attach** themselves to rocks using sticky threads made from fluid inside their body.

Scallops

Speedy scallops open and clap their shells shut to move. This **shoots out water** and propels them along, making them quicker than most bivalves.

The giant clam is the LARGEST BIVALVE in the WORLD!

Giant clam

Cockles

If predators come too close, cockles use their muscly "foot" to **dig** themselves into the sand and escape.

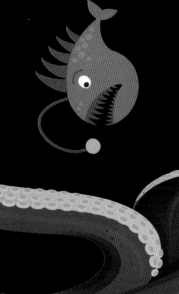

The tiny bobtail squid is less than 2.5 cm (1 in) long – the same size as a postage stamp!

I can grow to the length of a bus!

Super squid

The colossal squid hides in deep Antarctic waters. It is rarely seen, even though it is the largest living **invertebrate**, and the biggest squid on Earth.

Water whopper!

The colossal squid is the largest species in the **cephalopod** family, which has more than 800 different octopus, squid, and cuttlefish.

Eye

This squid has the **biggest eyes** of any animal – each eye is bigger than a basketball!

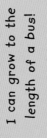

Beak

The colossal squid has two very long tentacles covered in **moving hooks**. These are perfect for grabbing prey, which the squid shreds using its **beak**.

Arm

Tentacle

Hooks on the tentacle hold the fish tight.

Spot the difference

Sometimes people think that octopuses and squid are the same animal. They both belong to the cephalopod family and have lots in common, but they also have many **differences…**

	Octopus	Squid
Number of species:	300	298
Arms:	8	8
Tentacles:	0	2
Head shape:	Round	Triangular
Fins:	0	2 on head
Size:	Up to 9 m (29 ft)	Up to 20 m (65 ft)
Shell:	None	Bony form called pen
Habitat:	Ocean floor	Open ocean
Life expectancy:	3 years	5 years
Blood:	Blue	Blue

Enormous octopus

Get counting, because this giant octopus has loads of **body parts**. It has three hearts, and more than 2,000 suckers covering its eight arms!

Octopuses probably see in black and white.

Giant Pacific octopus

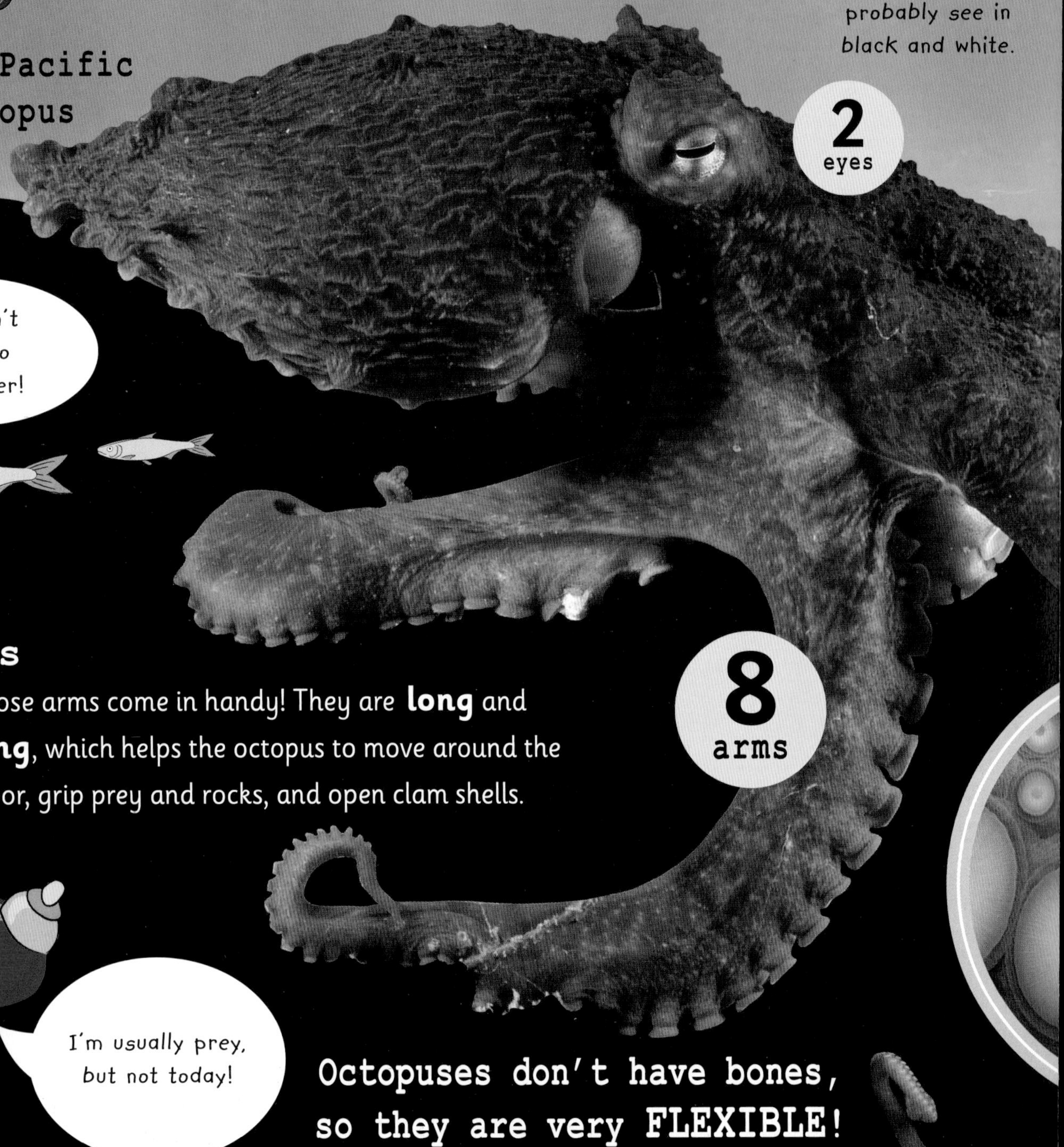

2 eyes

We don't want to be dinner!

Arms

All those arms come in handy! They are **long** and **strong**, which helps the octopus to move around the seafloor, grip prey and rocks, and open clam shells.

8 arms

I'm usually prey, but not today!

Octopuses don't have bones, so they are very FLEXIBLE!

Big beast

The **giant Pacific octopus** is bigger than any other type of octopus. It is easy to spot because it is bright red and has a huge head. It moves by pumping water through its soft body.

A deep-sea diver meets a giant Pacific octopus.

Octopuses hide in their surroundings by changing colour.

Octopuses get their name from the Latin word "OCTO", meaning "EIGHT".

2,000
suckers

Suckers

This octopus has about 2,000 **sticky suckers** on its eight arms – that's around 250 suckers on each arm! Suckers are super-strong and sensitive, providing the octopus with its sense of taste and smell.

Hearts

The octopus has **two hearts**, which transport blood to the gills used for breathing. It also has a **third heart**, which keeps blood flowing around the rest of the body.

3
hearts

Sea snails and slugs

Slimy snails and slugs don't just live in your garden, many have **underwater homes**.

Big family

All slugs and snails are members of the **gastropod** family. Most gastropods live in the ocean. They crawl along the seafloor on a muscular "foot", or float on ocean currents. Many have hard shells for protection.

Sea snails

These gastropods are easy to spot because they have **visible shells** that are usually spiral-shaped. Some sea snails hunt or scavenge for animals, such as worms, but others eat plants.

Some people call me "Triton's trumpet".

The sea butterfly is a tiny sea snail. It "flies" upside down through the water using its "foot" like a pair of wings.

One of the biggest snails in the sea is the giant triton. It has an excellent sense of smell, which it uses to detect prey, such as starfish.

The cone snail hunts fish. Its deadly venom paralyses prey and stops it from swimming away.

Sea slugs

Some types of sea snails evolved into sea slugs. Over millions of years, they **lost their shells**. Most sea slugs are brightly coloured and eat fish or plants.

Sea angels are speedy swimmers. This transparent sea slug looks a bit like an angel flying through the water.

I like to eat sea butterflies for my dinner.

The blue dragon matches the tropical waters that it lives in. This sea slug is small, but deadly! It take venom from its prey, and uses it against its predators.

With two long ears, the sea bunny resembles a rabbit. It is poisonous because it eats sea sponges that are full of toxic substances.

57

Marine reptiles

Marine reptiles like to live on **land** and in the **water**. Some spend their entire lives in the water, while others only sneak in to catch something for dinner.

Crocodiles lay their eggs on land.

Sea turtles were around at the same time as the dinosaurs!

Croc carriers

Most marine reptiles lay their **eggs** in **sandy places**. After they hatch, mother crocodiles carry their young gently to the water in their mouths. They can carry up to 15 hatchlings at the same time!

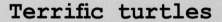

Terrific turtles

Sea turtles spend their whole lives at sea, and often travel long distances to find food. They can be found in almost **every ocean** in the world.

Home sweet home

Marine reptiles live in **watery places** around the world. Some live in fresh water like rivers, while others prefer salt water, such as the ocean. Some reptiles like water that is a mixture of both, this is called "brackish" water.

Salty sneezers

Living in salty water means many reptiles eat **too much salt**. But, they have clever ways to get rid of it. Marine iguanas sneeze it out!

Excuse me!

Slithery swimmers

Seas snakes have long, flat bodies that are perfect for **gliding** through the ocean. They can hold their breath underwater for hours at a time.

Some sea snakes hunt for food in coral reefs.

Seabed snackers

Most reptiles find their food underwater. Marine iguanas **grip** the seabed with their claws and use their snouts to scrape algae from rocks to eat.

Terrific turtles

Sea turtles have existed for more than **100 million** years and once lived alongside the dinosaurs! Today, these remarkable reptiles travel long distances to breed and feed.

A smooth SHELL and long FLIPPERS make the turtle a SUPERB SWIMMER.

Flipper

Strong swimmer

Turtles spend most of their lives in water and have a strong sense of direction. They can **hold their breath** underwater for up to seven hours at a time!

Turtles can live for 50 or even 100 YEARS!

Cleaner fish eat the algae and dead skin from turtle shells.

Shell

Leatherback turtle

Meet the world's **biggest sea turtle** – it can grow to the size of a small car! Instead of a hard shell, the leatherback turtle has leathery skin. It will swim from Asia to the USA in search of food.

Leatherback turtle

Green turtle

Green turtle

Unlike other turtles, the adult green turtle doesn't eat meat. Instead, it eats a diet of **seagrass** and **algae**. It gets its name from its green body fat.

We're not rocks, we're turtles!

In 1503, Christopher Columbus thought an island of turtles was a mound of rocks!

What are those strange rocks ahead?

61

Fishy friends

Fish are covered in **scales**, and use **fins** and **tails** for swimming. Although they come in all different shapes and sizes, they share the same basic features.

Tail powers the fish through the water.

Dorsal fins on top help the fish to stay balanced.

Scales are tiny, protective plates that cover the body.

Pelvic fins on the underside help the fish to change direction.

I'm not the first fish, but I am so old that I'm fossilised!

The FIRST fish lived

This bullet-shaped tuna fish is speedy!

Telling tails

Look at the **shapes** of fish tails and discover how fish swim through the seas.

Special shape

Many fish are super swimmers because of their **streamlined** shape. Their smooth bodies move easily through the water.

Pectoral fins on the side help the fish to turn around.

Gills absorb oxygen from the water. Fish use gills to breathe.

Crescent tail

A tail shaped like a crescent moon is the perfect shape for high-speed **swimming**.

Paddle tail

A tail shaped like the paddle of a rowing boat is used to make **speedy attacks** on prey.

Forked tail

A tail shaped like a fork allows the fish to easily move around in **all directions**.

about 500 **MILLION** years ago.

Fabulous fish

There are more than 32,000 types of fish. They are divided into **three main groups** depending on their body type and skeleton.

Bony fish

Most fish are bony fish. They have an internal **skeleton** made of bone that is strong, but light, so they can swim easily. The strong skeleton supports flexible fins, for easy movement. Most bony fish have an air bladder inside to help them float.

Flying fish

I'm a bony fish. I use my large, flexible fins as "wings" to escape danger and "fly" out of the sea at high speeds.

Dwarf goby

I'm the world's heaviest bony fish. I'm as big and heavy as a family car.

I'm among the smallest fish in the sea. I'm about the same size as your fingernail.

Sunfish

Eagle ray

Jawless fish

Jawless fish were the first fish on Earth. **Lampreys** clamp their round mouths and hooked teeth onto prey, and guzzle the blood – just like blood-sucking vampires! In addition to jaws, jawless fish are missing fins and a stomach.

Sharks and rays are cartilaginous fish.

Teeth

Eel-like lampreys and hagfish are the only living jawless fish.

Cartilaginous fish

The skeleton of cartilaginous fish is not made of bones, it's made of a soft, flexible substance, called **cartilage**. These fish don't have air bladders, so they must keep swimming or they will sink.

Lamprey

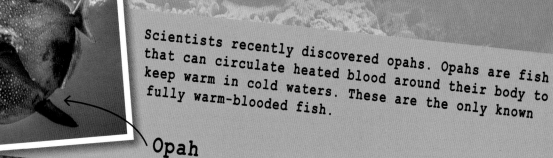

Scientists recently discovered opahs. Opahs are fish that can circulate heated blood around their body to keep warm in cold waters. These are the only known fully warm-blooded fish.

Opah

Superb seahorses

With their horse-like heads and curly tails, seahorses look **strange**. They are closely related to sea dragons and pipefish — what a weird family!

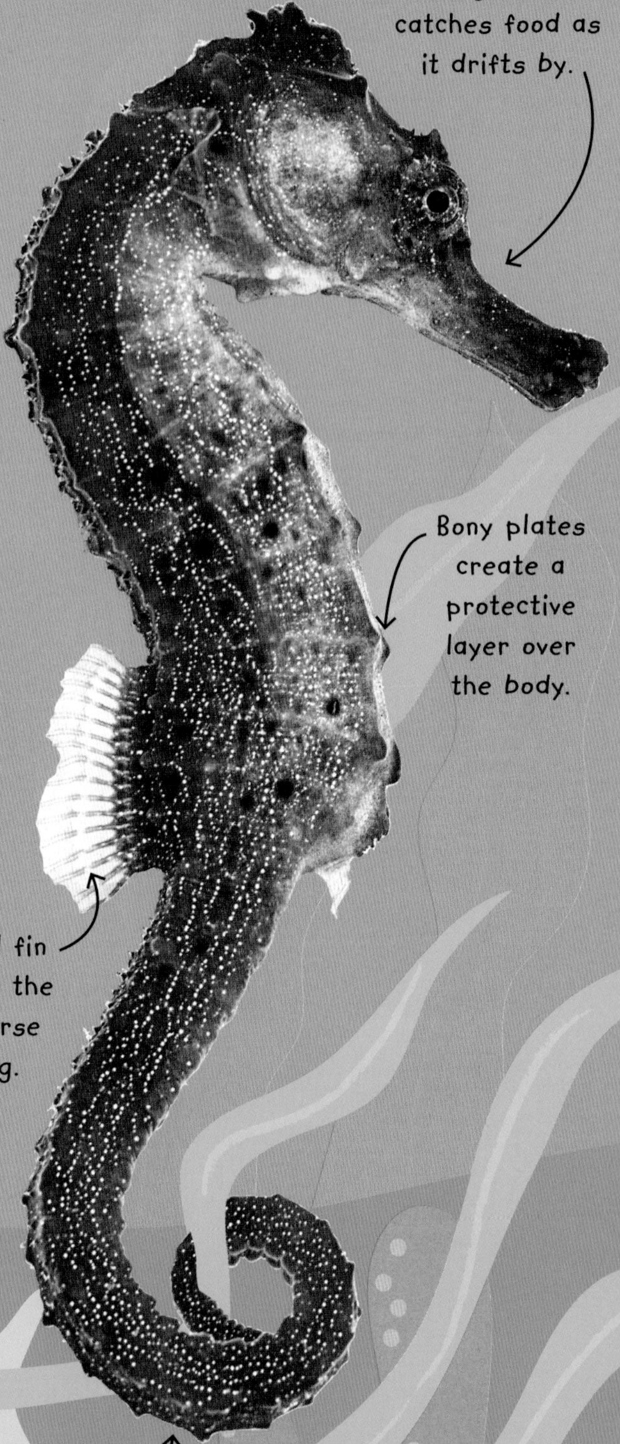

Long snout catches food as it drifts by.

Bony plates create a protective layer over the body.

Dorsal fin pushes the seahorse along.

Seahorses

Although they may not look like it, seahorses are actually **fish**. They keep themselves upright and swim poorly, but have plates all over their bodies to protect them from predators.

Curly tail grips hold of seaweed.

Seahorses use their TUBE-LIKE mouths

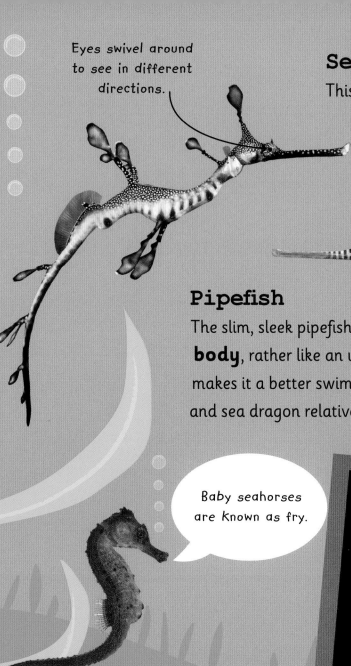

Eyes swivel around to see in different directions.

Sea dragon

This little **dragon-like** creature is a relative of the seahorse. Brightly coloured and frilly, it blends in so well with seaweed that predators struggle to spot it.

Pipefish

The slim, sleek pipefish has a long, **streamlined body**, rather like an underwater worm. This makes it a better swimmer than its seahorse and sea dragon relatives.

Long, thin body.

Baby seahorses are known as fry.

I carry up to 2,000 babies in my pouch!

In the animal kingdom, females usually have the babies. But for seahorses, the males go through pregnancy. They keep the eggs in a tummy pouch until they hatch.

to **SUCK** up food.

> My close cousin is the seahorse.

Leafy sea dragons

Living off the shores of southern Australia, the leafy sea dragon floats through the ocean **disguised** as drifting seaweed.

Leafy look

Leafy sea dragons get their name from the **green, leaf-like** pieces of skin hanging from their heads, bodies, and tails. This unique look means they can hide in seaweed and seagrass without being seen by predators or prey.

Clever camouflage

Sea dragons can **change colour** to blend in with their surroundings. Their diet and age can affect how good they are at changing colour.

Male sea dragons carry eggs

Sloooooowwww motion travel

Long snout

Pectoral fin

Dorsal fin

Curled tail

Slow swimmers

Leafy sea dragons aren't in a rush! They move through the ocean at super-slow speeds. **Pectoral** fins on their heads help them steer, while **dorsal** fins help them move along.

Sea dragons use their tube-like snouts as straws, to suck up tiny sea creatures.

Secret defence

Their bodies are covered in protective **plates** and sharp **spines** for self-defence.

I have no teeth, so I swallow my prey whole!

stuck to their bodies!

Sleek sharks

Sharks are super hunters that have ruled the ocean for **millions** of years. These speedy swimmers have a big bite, and can smell blood in the water from far away.

Powerful tail propels the shark quickly through the water.

Fins help sharks move easily in the ocean.

Dwarf lantern shark

Little and large

There are over 510 species of sharks alive today, and they come in **all shapes and sizes**. Whale sharks are the size of a bus, while dwarf lantern sharks could fit into the palm of your hand.

Longnose saw shark

The longnose saw shark has a snout like a **chainsaw**, with long **barbels** hanging off it. These are special organs that can detect prey on the ocean floor.

Hammerhead shark

This shark has a **wide head** and excellent eyesight. It has nostrils and eyes on the sides of its head to help it find prey.

Barbel

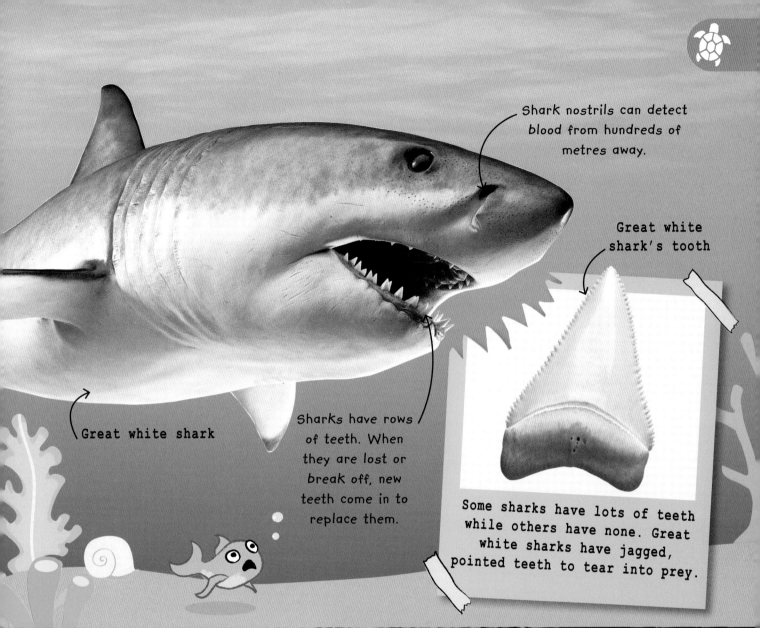

Shark nostrils can detect blood from hundreds of metres away.

Great white shark's tooth

Great white shark

Sharks have rows of teeth. When they are lost or break off, new teeth come in to replace them.

Some sharks have lots of teeth while others have none. Great white sharks have jagged, pointed teeth to tear into prey.

Cookiecutter shark

The cookiecutter shark is around 50 cm (20 in) long — that's the length of the average human baby at birth. This small shark likes to sneak up on large creatures and bite **circular chunks** out of them.

Greenland shark

This huge shark is the oldest living animal with a backbone and can live for more than 400 years. It swims slowly through cold **Arctic seas**, is blind, and hunts only by smell.

Rays and skates

These famously **flat fish** have long tails and wing-shaped fins. Some of them hide by burying themselves in the sand.

RAYS and SKATES are closely related to SHARKS.

Stingray or skate?

How can you tell the difference between a stingray and a skate? As its name suggests, the stingray has a long tail with a **venomous stinger** for self-defence. The skate has a much thicker, shorter tail than the stingray. It does not have a stinger and is harmless to humans.

Stingray tail

Skate tail

Record-breaker

The **common skate** is the heaviest and largest skate in the world. This superb swimmer eats crabs on the seabed, and fish swimming in the open ocean.

Spiky sea creature

Living up to its name, the **thorny skate** is covered in spines, which make it look like a prehistoric dinosaur.

The giant manta ray is the world's BIGGEST ray.

Manta ray

Mouth

Lobe

Chimaeras

Rays and skates are **related** to a group of fish called chimaeras. These fish look quite similar to one another, with large heads, round snouts, long bodies, and mostly smooth skin with no scales.

Open wide!

The **manta ray** has a long tail, but no stinger. This gentle giant swims along with its mouth open to catch small fish and plankton.

Manta rays are called "devil fish" because their lobes look like devilish horns.

Chimaeras live in every ocean except the Atlantic!

Plough-nosed chimaera

Super-stinger

Treading on a **southern stingray** will cause a painful sting, but this ray won't hurt you on purpose. It rests in the sand by day, and hunts molluscs and worms by night.

Diving dolphins

Dolphins are **cetaceans** – mammals, just like us, but they live in the ocean. They are known for being clever, chatty, and cute! What's not to like?

A dolphin powers through the water by moving its tail up and down.

Thick as thieves

Dolphins love company, so they live in close groups, called **pods**. The pod will swim, hunt, and play together.

The dorsal fin helps the dolphin to balance.

We've developed our own "language", using a mix of clicks, squeaks, and whistles.

Click!

Front flippers allow the dolphin to steer and change direction.

Playtime

Dolphins are friendly and **playful** animals. They like swimming near boats and leaping out of the water together.

When they fancy a feast, dolphins work together to herd groups of fish into one place. They surround them, so that the fish cannot escape!

Caring and sharing

Dolphins are **kind** to one another. They share food, raise their young together, and protect each other. Dolphins have also been known to come to the rescue when people need help.

Half asleep

When sleeping, dolphins rest only **one side of their brain** at a time. This allows them to stay alert and watch out for sharks.

zzzzzZZZZZZ

Squeak!

I keep one eye open when I'm asleep.

Click, click, squeak, whistle!

Wonderful whales

Whales are **enormous**! These social creatures have bulky bodies, big bellies, and incredibly powerful tails.

Beluga whale

I live in frozen Arctic waters.

Marine mammals

Whales are mammals, so they have to come to the surface for air. **Blowholes** on the top of their heads are like giant nostrils to help them breathe.

The wrinkly **sperm whale** is large and loud! It makes noisy clicks that can be heard 15 km (10 miles) away.

Sperm whale

The sperm whale's huge nose helps it make loud sounds.

The BOWHEAD WHALE is thought to be one

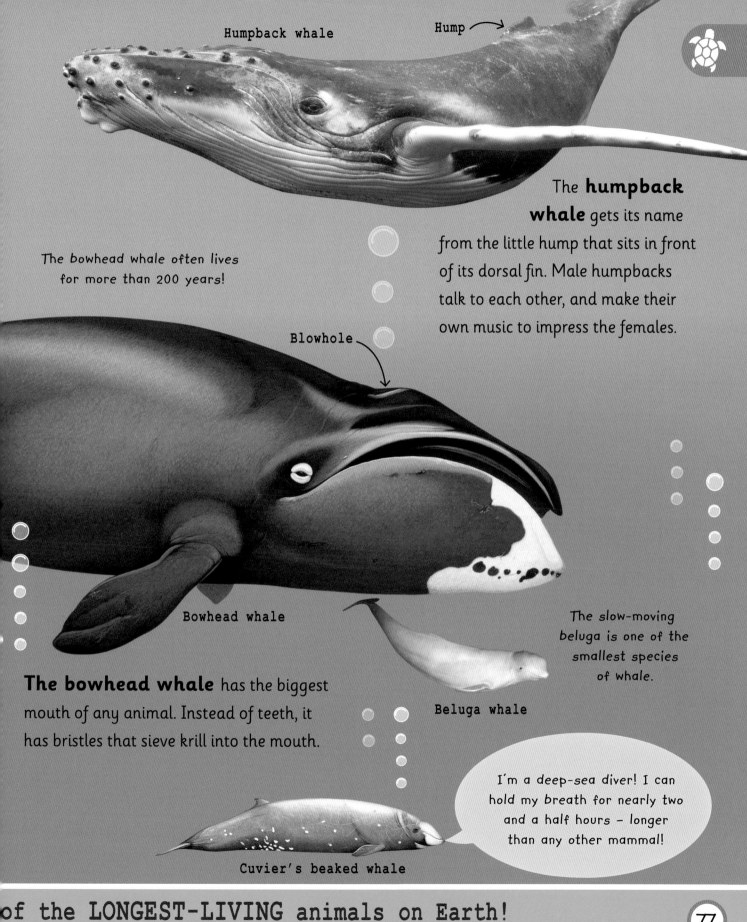

Humpback whale

Hump

The **humpback whale** gets its name from the little hump that sits in front of its dorsal fin. Male humpbacks talk to each other, and make their own music to impress the females.

The bowhead whale often lives for more than 200 years!

Blowhole

Bowhead whale

The slow-moving beluga is one of the smallest species of whale.

Beluga whale

The bowhead whale has the biggest mouth of any animal. Instead of teeth, it has bristles that sieve krill into the mouth.

I'm a deep-sea diver! I can hold my breath for nearly two and a half hours – longer than any other mammal!

Cuvier's beaked whale

of the LONGEST-LIVING animals on Earth!

Big blue whale

Meet the **largest** and **heaviest** creature on the planet! This whale is the super-sized star of the oceans and breaks all kinds of records for being big.

Magnificent mammal

The blue whale is the largest animal ever to have lived – it's **bigger** than the **dinosaurs**! This ocean giant can be found swimming in every ocean except for the Arctic Ocean.

The tail has two lobes, called "flukes".

Flukes move up and down, powering the whale through the ocean.

Krill

30.5 m (100 ft)

This whale eats four tonnes of krill every day!

An adult blue whale is the same length as SEVEN CARS!

Growing up fast

Baby blue whales, called calves, are the **largest offspring** of any species. They feed on their mother's milk. Calves drink so much milk that they gain the equivalent weight of five young children every day!

Baby blue whales learn to swim minutes after they are born.

Their skin markings are as unique as your fingerprints.

The spray from a blue whale's blowhole squirts up to 9 m (30 ft) high – the same height as two giraffes!

They have long, streamlined bodies.

Each eye is the size of a grapefruit.

Giant flippers help the whale move in different directions.

At 150 tonnes (165 tons), the blue whale is almost as heavy as a JUMBO JET!

Blue whale songs can be heard for miles around!

Real unicorn horns for sale

In the past, hunters pretended the narwhal tusk was a unicorn horn and sold it for lots of money.

Unicorn of the sea

The legendary **narwhal** is known as the "unicorn of the sea" because of its spiral tusk. However, it is not a mythical creature, but a real whale that lives in the icy waters of the Arctic Ocean.

Tusk

Experts think male narwhals have tusks to attract females, find food, and fight each other.

Tremendous tooth

The male narwhal is unlike any other marine creature because it has an incredibly long tusk. This tusk is really a **giant tooth** – the only kind of tooth narwhals have. Some males grow two tusks, and some female narwhals grow a small tusk, too.

The narwhal tusk can reach 3 m (10 ft) long – about the same length as a small car!

Breath of fresh air

Narwhals need to come up for air – just like other mammals. They poke their **blowhole** through the ice before plunging back under the icy ocean.

Narwhals can hold their breath for up to 25 minutes.

Seafood menu

Narwhals eat a range of delicious seafood, including Arctic cod, Greenland halibut, squid, and shrimp. They have no teeth inside their mouths, so they swallow food in **one gulp**.

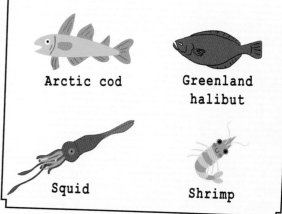

Arctic cod

Greenland halibut

Squid

Shrimp

Deep freeze

Life is tough in the Arctic. Narwhals don't migrate like other whales. Instead, they survive the long, cold winters by moving nearby to deeper water, and hiding **under the ice** for months at a time.

Safety in numbers

Narwhals are hunted by polar bears and walruses. They swim in **groups** of around 10 to 20, and sometimes up to 100, which makes it more difficult for a predator to target just one whale.

Walruses, seals, and sea lions

Pinnipeds is a group of water-living mammals, which includes seals, walruses, and sea lions. They move awkwardly on land, but glide through water. All pinnipeds have a thick layer of fat, called **blubber**.

Walruses

Walruses have **enormous tusks**. They use them to fight, to haul their big bodies out of the water, and to break breathing holes into ice from underwater.

Seals

The largest group of pinnipeds is true, or **earless**, seals. They do have ears, but they are hidden under their skin. These seals move on land by wriggling on their bellies.

Baby harp seals live in cold waters. Their fluffy, white fur helps them to hide in the snow.

Sea lions

Unlike seals, sea lions have **external ears**. These speedy swimmers have long flippers that help them "walk" on land.

The bearded seal has sensitive whiskers, which it uses to feel for prey, such as crabs, on the ocean floor.

Male hooded seals have a stretchy red "hood" in their nose that inflates like a balloon.

GRUNT! GRUNT!

The largest of all seals, an elephant seal can grow to 6 m (20 ft) long – that's as long as a great white shark!

Playful penguins

These birds **can't fly**, but they don't have any trouble moving around their snowy home.

Some penguins slide across the ice on their bellies.

To move quickly, penguins can leap, or "porpoise", out of the water.

Speedy swimmers

Penguins are **naturals** in the water, spending most of their lives in the ocean. Many penguins are fast swimmers, which can be useful when hunting for food, such as squid.

A sleek shape helps penguins glide as they swim.

Squid

Oh no!

They use their stiff flippers to steer.

Land huddle

Emperor penguins come onto land when they are ready to **lay eggs** and raise chicks. The male penguins keep the eggs warm, protecting them with their feathery bodies until they hatch.

Once hatched, emperor penguin chicks huddle together in groups while their parents catch food.

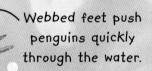

Webbed feet push penguins quickly through the water.

No one will *see* me in my new disguise!

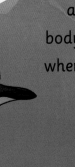

Protective colours

Their black and white feathers are actually a type of **camouflage**. A black back and body means they blend in with the dark ocean when seen from above, and a white belly helps them blend in with the sunny surface of the ocean when seen from below.

Soaring seabirds

Seabirds fly out to sea and **scan the waves** from high above. Some hunt by skimming across the waters surface, others dive deep beneath the waves to search for food.

> I live in a group called a "colony".

Born survivors

Seabirds have **special features**, which help them to survive at sea. They have glands to filter out the salt from sea water, and webbed feet to paddle with. Some have specially shaped wings that help them swim, while others have wide wings for long journeys.

Red-billed gull

This seabird lives in **large nesting colonies** by the shore. Its food includes fish, crabs, and even food scraps!

White-tailed sea eagle

This bird swoops down and snatches up fish in its **sharp claws**. It also has a huge wingspan that is wider than most people are tall!

Artic tern

The Arctic tern flies farther than any other bird. Every year, this tiny bird travels from its breeding ground in the **Arctic** to its summer feeding ground in the **Antarctic**.

Arctic

Antarctic

Sailors believed that seeing an albatross was a sign of good luck.

Albatross

The wandering albatross is the biggest seabird. It glides across the ocean and **follows ships** in search of food.

We love you albatross!

Brown pelican

The pelican dives down and collects fish and water in its **beak**. It then spits out the water and gobbles up the fish.

87

Ocean

environments

There is a huge **variety of habitats** in the ocean. Jump into sun-kissed tropical waters and dip your toe in icy polar seas. Experience colourful coral reefs, dark kelp forests, and swampy mangroves on this magical tour of magnificent marine kingdoms.

Seashores

Seashores are battered by winds and waves, and are swept by the tides. Plants and animals must be able to survive these **challenging** conditions.

Oystercatcher

Whelks

Red knot

Barnacles

We spend half our time ou of water!

Mussels

Limpets

Are you shore?

There are four main types of seashore:

Sandy

Many seashores are covered in grains of sand.

Pebbly

Some shorelines have small pebbles or shingle.

Muddy

Muddy shores are made up of mud and clay.

Rocky

Some coastal areas are surrounded by rocky cliffs.

Mole crabs dig themselves into the sand backwards, while keeping their eyes on the sea to find food.

Let's dig!

Rock pools are pockets of water left behind by the outgoing tide. Some creatures live in the pools.

In the zone

The **intertidal zone** is an area between the high and low-tide marks. During high tide, the zone is covered by water. At low tide, it is mostly dry. Creatures that live here have to cope with both wet and dry conditions. The **splash zone** is just past the high-tide area, and can be hit by high winds and crashing waves in storms.

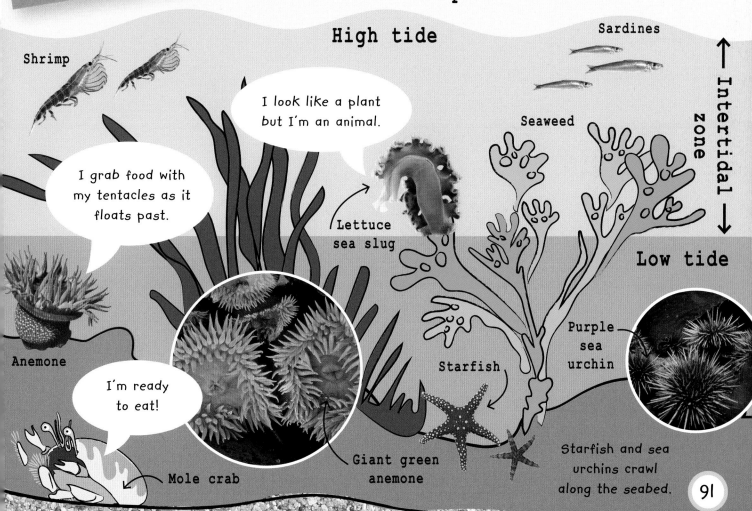

Splash zone

High tide

Sardines

Shrimp

I look like a plant but I'm an animal.

Seaweed

I grab food with my tentacles as it floats past.

Lettuce sea slug

Intertidal zone

Low tide

Anemone

Purple sea urchin

Starfish

I'm ready to eat!

Giant green anemone

Mole crab

Starfish and sea urchins crawl along the seabed.

Coastal habitats

They might look peaceful, but some of Earth's **busiest** habitats are found on coastlines.

Estuaries

An estuary is the **watery area** where a river finishes its journey and meets the sea. It's where fresh water from the river and salt water from the sea mix.

Mud flats

Mud flats are large areas of **flat, muddy land**. They flood when the tide comes in, so they can only be seen at low tide. Muddy materials and tiny particles from rivers and seas are left behind when the tide goes out.

When the tide goes out, the mud can smell of rotten eggs! This smell is caused by bacteria in the mud.

Salt marshes

Salt marshes are areas of land that are sometimes covered by salt water. **Mud flats** can become salt marshes. In places where tides can't wash the soil away, plants can grow. These plants hold the soil in place and allow even more plants to form.

Lagoons

Lagoons are pools of shallow water that have been cut off from the sea by island reefs or bars of sand. These **still**, **isolated** areas of water have no tides or currents.

Plants and tall grasses are the perfect hiding places for tiny wildlife.

Saltmarsh caterpillar

Mouse ear snail

Lots of worms, insects, snails, and shrimp live in salt marshes. They attract hungry fish and birds.

Common redshank

93

Mangroves

Mangroves are trees and shrubs that grow along the shores of warm, tropical oceans. They form beautiful **mangrove forests** that are partly underwater. Many creatures live and hunt in the branches and roots of mangrove trees.

Indian **bengal tigers** hunt in swampy mangroves. They swim to hunt their prey.

Fiddler crabs live on the shore. Male crabs each have one large claw, which they use to defend their territory.

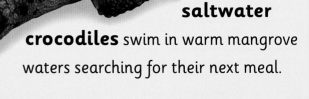

At high tide, **saltwater crocodiles** swim in warm mangrove waters searching for their next meal.

Many animals depend on

Brown-winged kingfisher

The soil in mangrove forests is thick and airless. Some mangrove trees grow their roots above ground, which helps them to take in oxygen from the air.

Mudskippers are fish that live in burrows in the mud. They use their fins to skip along the surface.

Archerfish squirt jets of water at insects resting on mangrove leaves. This knocks the insects into the water, so they can be eaten.

mangroves for FOOD and SHELTER.

Seagrass meadows

When you think of a meadow, you probably think of land, but there are also huge fields of **underwater grass**. These are called "seagrass meadows" and they are home to many incredible animals.

Sunlit gardens

Seagrass meadows need **lots of light** to grow. They are found on the coast where the water isn't too deep, which means it's easier for the sunlight to reach the grass.

Some seagrasses have long, thin leaves – like spaghetti! Other grasses have short, fat leaves.

Shoal grass

Star grass

Common seahorse

Hold on tight!

Using its tail, the seahorse **clings** onto the seagrass to avoid being swept away.

Super seagrasses

Seagrasses help keep the sea **clean**. They filter the water around them, and stop the seabed from being washed away by the currents.

Sea cows are the ONLY VEGETARIAN marine mammals.

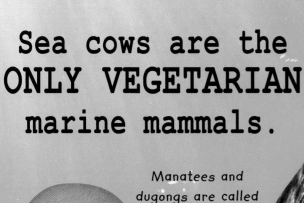

Manatees and dugongs are called "sea cows".

Dugong

Manatee

Seagrass meadows are home to thousands of baby fish, so they are often called "nurseries".

Big eater
The **manatee** eats huge amounts of seagrass. It grazes on grass for up to eight hours a day.

Fabulous flowers
Seagrasses looks a bit like seaweed, but they are more like the **plants** found on land. They have seeds, fruits, and pollen. Seagrass flowers are rarely seen because they only flower for a short time.

Mediterranean seagrass

Greater pipefish

Hide and seek
The long, thin pipefish is a similar size and shape to some seagrass, so it can easily **hide** from passing predators.

Kelp forests

In cool, shallow, coastal waters around the world grows a special type of **seaweed**, called "kelp". Where it grows thickly, kelp can form spectacular underwater forests, which provide welcome shelter for many marine visitors.

Giant kelp is the world's largest seaweed. It can reach 45 m (148 ft) high – that's about the height of a four-storey building!

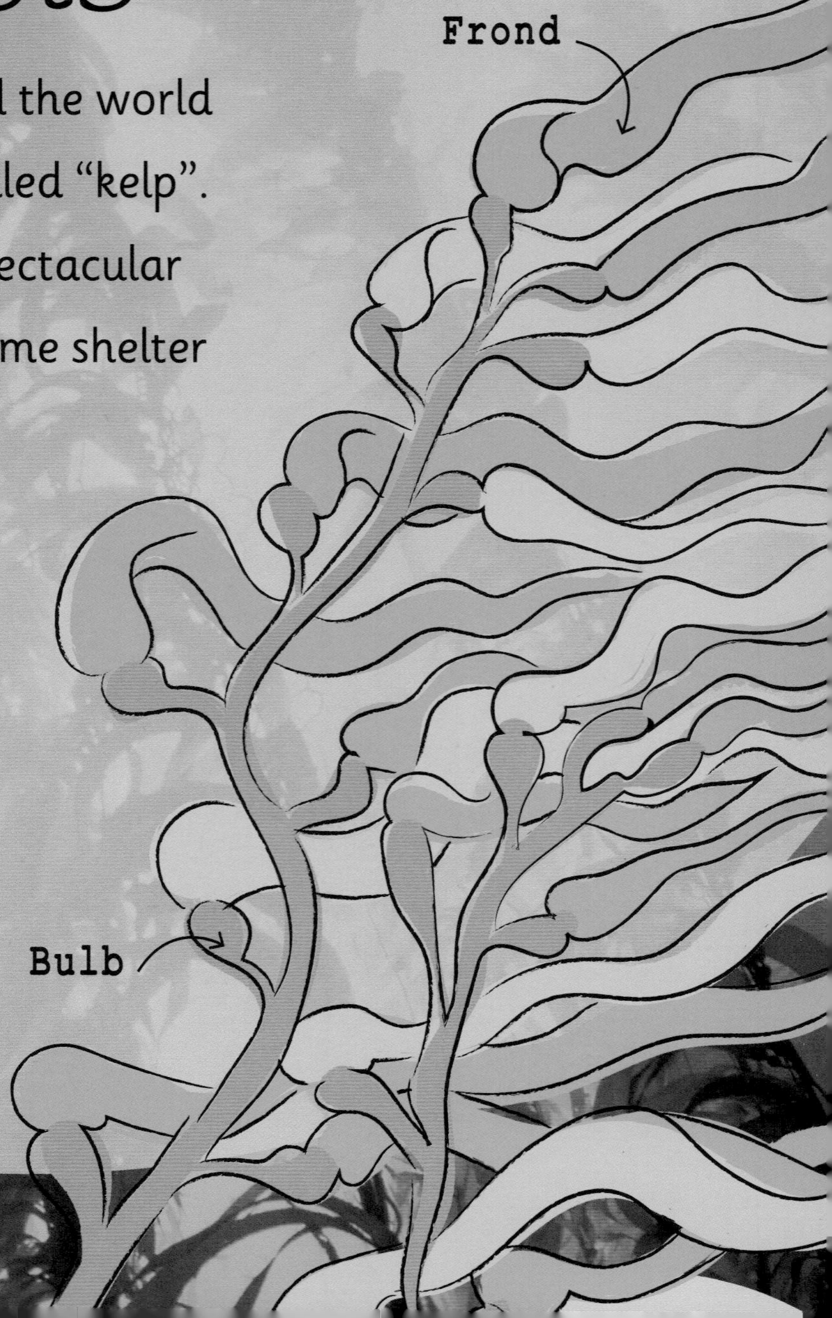

Leaf-like fronds grow from the stipe.

Frond

Bulb

Air-filled bulbs make the kelp float.

Seahorse

Leopard shark

Kelp can grow by more than half a metre every day – that's the length of a baby!

The stipe is the kelp's trunk.

Holdfast roots anchor the kelp to rocks on the seafloor.

Stipe

Holdfast

Sea urchins have sharp teeth on their underside, which they use to eat away at the kelp's holdfast. Otters protect the kelp by eating the urchins.

Purple sea urchins

Sea lion

Thick areas of kelp make good hiding places for sneaky **sea lions** when they are hunting for fish to eat.

Sea otters rest by wrapping themselves in fronds and floating on the surface of the water. The kelp stops them from drifting away.

Sea otters

Sea anemone

Coral reefs

Coral reefs are found in tropical seas around the world. These colourful underwater **habitats** are bursting with marine life. Come on, dive in!

I can see all the colours of the rainbow down here!

Creating coral
Coral reefs are made up of tiny creatures called "polyps". Thousands live together forming huge, hard **structures** called "corals".

Protected polyps
Polyps are teeny-tiny marine life protected by tough shells. When they die, their skeletons stack up on top of each other.

Red Sea fan coral

Soft coral

Sea whip

Large star coral

The GREAT BARRIER REEF

Remarkable reef

The Great Barrier Reef is huge! It's made up of more than **3,000 coral reefs**, and stretches for thousands of miles across the Coral Sea, off the northeast coast of Australia.

Underwater visitors

Laws control where tourists can dive, sail, and fish to make sure that coral reefs do not become any **more damaged**.

The outer reef is perfect for scuba diving. It is deeper than the inner reef, and home to larger fish.

The Great Barrier Reef is home to around 600 species of colourful coral.

Staghorn coral

Gorgonian coral

Brain coral

The inner reef is sheltered and shallow.

is the WORLD'S BIGGEST REEF.

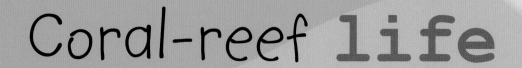

Coral-reef life

Coral reefs are found in less than one per cent of the ocean, but they provide shelter and safety for **25 per cent** of marine life! Let's meet the reef creatures who thrive in this rocky, rainbow world.

Sea cow

Scientists estimate that at least one million different animal species live on coral reefs.

Bright and busy

Coral reefs are **full of life**. Sea cows and dolphins swim past sneaky sharks, flapping rays, and shiny shoals of fish. Along the seabed, sea snakes watch out for prey, while families of fish feast on chunks of coral.

Damselfish

Pink skunk clownfish

Sea snake

Feather star

Sea anemone

Flatworm

Brittle star

Clownfish

CORAL REEFS are known as "the

The enormous manta ray is cleaned by smaller fish.

Manta ray

Sea turtle

Blacktip reef shark

The barracuda uses its strong jaws and sharp teeth to seize prey.

Barracuda

Sponge

Sea urchin

Lionfish

Angelfish

I match my home. Hiding on the *seabed* means I can *surprise* my prey!

Blue-ringed octopus

Wobbegong shark

RAINFORESTS of the seas".

Natural reefs

Not all reefs are made of coral. There are different kinds found all around the world. These natural **underwater barriers** can be formed from rocks or even sea creatures.

Rocky reefs

Rocks beneath the water can become a haven for wildlife. Seaweed and sea anemones attach to the rocks, while fish take shelter in the **cracks** and **holes** made by **crashing waves**.

Oyster reefs

Oysters fuse to hard surfaces and each other to form a reef. Oyster reefs shelter sea creatures, clean the ocean, and act as barriers to **prevent erosion** from storms and tides.

Oyster

What is a reef?

A reef is a **ridge** that is found at, or just below, the **surface** of the ocean. Reefs attract plenty of marine creatures, in search of food or shelter.

Serpulid reefs

Serpulid tubeworms gather to form nests. Their resulting reef looks like a giant **aquatic bush**, where marine life comes to explore.

Serpulid tubeworm

Flame shell reefs

The flame shell is a fiery orange clam that **builds nests** from shells and stones. Hundreds of nests join to make a dense reef on the seabed.

Flame shell

Artificial reefs

Reefs can be artificial, which means they are **made by humans**. We have been building them for thousands of years!

Reasons for artificial reefs

Reefs act as **safety barriers** to protect coastlines from storms and erosion. They can make excellent habitats for marine life.

Man-made structures are used to make reefs in the ocean.

Reef balls

Concrete reef balls are covered in holes and dropped into the sea for wildlife to live in. They are a **perfect playground** for fish and other sea life.

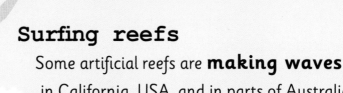

Surfing reefs

Some artificial reefs are **making waves** in California, USA, and in parts of Australia. Underwater structures have been designed to create the best ocean waves for surfers.

Sunken ships

Old ships make great artificial reefs. *USS Spiegel Grove* became the world's largest artificial reef when it was sunk off the Florida Keys, USA, in 2002. The reef attracts divers and **marine life**, including schools of tropical fish. Natural corals will gradually cover the ship.

USS Spiegel Grove

Coral grows on a sunken Jeep at Malapascua Island, Cebu, Philippines.

Sunken truck tyres help enrich and repair the damaged reefs at Malapascua Island.

Icy waters

The Arctic and Antarctic are the **coldest places** on Earth and the ocean around them is freezing, too. These waters are so cold that ice can form.

Arctic

Equator

Antarctic

The coldest areas of the ocean are far away from the equator.

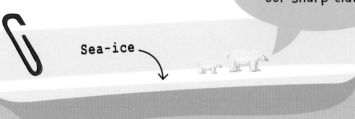

Sea-ice

We grip the ice with our sharp claws.

Sea-ice

When sea water freezes it is called "sea-ice". A thick, floating **layer of ice** can form on the ocean's surface. This ice can be so thick that animals can walk on it.

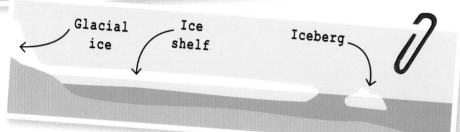

Glacial ice

Ice shelf

Iceberg

Ice shelves

When fresh water freezes it forms "glacial ice". This ice forms over land, and can grow until it reaches the coastline. When the ice pushes out **over the water**, it becomes an "ice shelf".

The Ward Hunt Ice Shelf in Canada is thousands of years old. It is the largest ice shelf in the Arctic.

The Ross Ice Shelf is the LARGEST ICE SHELF in Antarctica.

Icebergs

Huge chunks of ice can break off from an ice shelf and float away on ocean currents. These **blocks of ice** are called "icebergs". The largest part of an iceberg is hidden beneath the surface of the water.

Ships have to be careful not to crash into floating icebergs.

Flat iceberg

Wedge iceberg

Iceberg types

Icebergs come in different **shapes and sizes**. Some have steep sides and flat tops, others sloping sides and rounded tops.

Pinnacle iceberg

Iceberg B-15A is the largest iceberg ever recorded. When it broke away from the Ross Ice Shelf in 2000, it was larger than Jamaica. But it has since broken into smaller pieces.

We like to sleep on the floating ice.

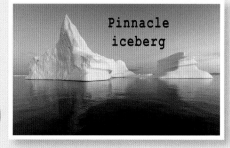
Ice arch

ICEBERGS can be as big as a small COUNTRY!

Arctic

Equator

Antarctic

Arctic waters

The Arctic Ocean is at the top of the Earth around the North Pole. With bitter winds and freezing temperatures, the animals there have **adapted** to survive.

The **polar bear** has a thick layer of body fat and a waterproof fur coat to keep it warm when swimming in the cold Arctic Ocean. In winter, the bear hunts seals on the ice.

The **narwhal** is a polar whale with a long, tusk-shaped tooth. It has a thick layer of fat under its skin to keep it warm.

The Arctic is COLD but temperatures there are gradually RISING.

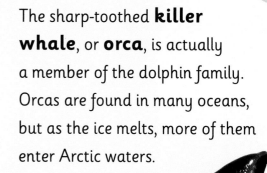

The sharp-toothed **killer whale**, or **orca**, is actually a member of the dolphin family. Orcas are found in many oceans, but as the ice melts, more of them enter Arctic waters.

As temperatures rise, polar animals are losing the ice they depend on to travel and hunt.

Like the narwhal, the **harp seal** has a layer of fat under the skin to keep it warm. It has flippers and smooth fur to help it swim fast and hunt in the cold waters.

Antarctic waters

Arctic

Antarctic

Equator

The Antarctic is the super-cold region at the very south of our planet. But it is full of **unique animals** that can survive the extreme cold.

Antarctic petrel

Emperor penguin

Only two species of penguin live in Antarctica full-time. The **Emperor** penguin is the biggest in the world, while the **Adélie** penguin is one of the smallest.

Adélie penguin

The **Antarctic petrel** is one of the few birds that's native to the Antarctic. Other species come and go throughout the year.

Antarctic krill are native to Antarctic waters. Many polar animals, such as whales and seals, feed on these tiny creatures.

Icefish have "antifreeze" in their blood to stop them from freezing in the cold water. Their blood is also white, instead of red like most animals.

Just how cold is the Antarctic?

Your freezer at home needs to stay at about -15°C (5°F). But in Antarctica, winter can be three times colder than that!

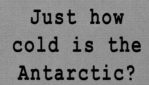

Hourglass dolphin

Some marine mammals, such as the **hourglass dolphin** and the **pygmy right whale**, have a layer of fat, called "blubber", to keep them warm.

Pygmy right whale

Weddell seal

Weddell seals live the furthest south of any mammal. They can stay under the water for around 70 minutes at a time!

The mysterious **colossal squid** roams deep Antarctic waters. Only a few have ever been seen, but they can grow to five times as big as a human adult!

Colossal squid

In the zone

We can split our deep ocean into five layers, from the **warm, sunlit surface**, to the **cold, dark depths** of the ocean.

Dolphins

Turtle

Seaweed

Orange jellyfish

School of sardines

Ocean sunfish

Plankton

Zone 1

The warmest and brightest zone is also the busiest. It is home to many plants and animals.

Zone 2

With only a bit of light, plants cannot survive here. Many creatures have big eyes to help them see better in the darkness.

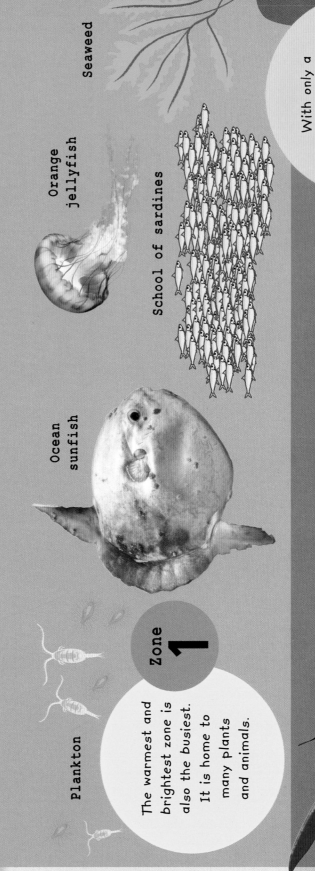

Hatchetfish

Lanternfish

Glass squid

Lanternshark

Sunlight zone
up to 200 m (650 ft) *below the surface*

Twilight zone
up to 1,000 m (3,280 ft)

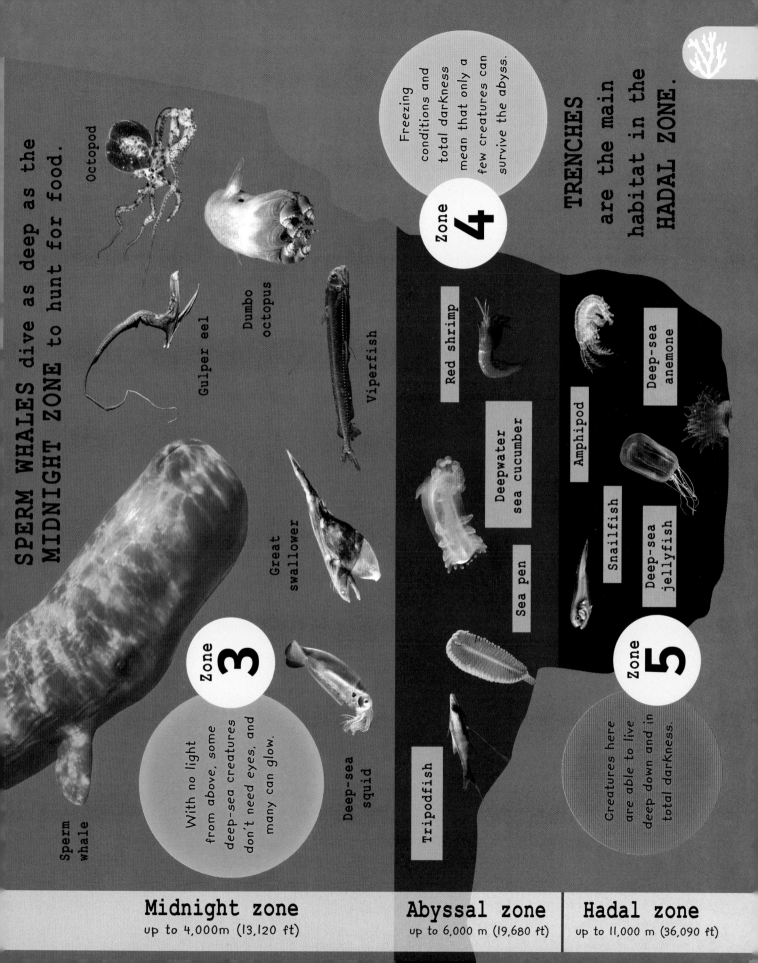

SPERM WHALES dive as deep as the MIDNIGHT ZONE to hunt for food.

Octopod

Gulper eel

Dumbo octopus

Viperfish

Great swallower

Sperm whale

Deep-sea squid

Zone 3

With no light from above, some deep-sea creatures don't need eyes, and many can glow.

Zone 4

Freezing conditions and total darkness mean that only a few creatures can survive the abyss.

TRENCHES are the main habitat in the HADAL ZONE.

Red shrimp

Deepwater sea cucumber

Sea pen

Tripodfish

Amphipod

Deep-sea anemone

Snailfish

Deep-sea jellyfish

Zone 5

Creatures here are able to live deep down and in total darkness.

Midnight zone
up to 4,000m (13,120 ft)

Abyssal zone
up to 6,000 m (19,680 ft)

Hadal zone
up to 11,000 m (36,090 ft)

Sunlight zone

Out in the open waters, beneath the surface, is the **highest layer** of the ocean. Welcome to the sunlight zone.

The sunlit surface

Sunlight warms the surface of the open ocean. Plants, algae, and plankton get their energy from the Sun — that's why this zone is so full of life!

Whale sharks swim with their mouths open searching for food.

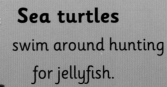

Sea turtles swim around hunting for jellyfish.

Most MARINE ANIMALS live in the SUNLIGHT ZONE.

Sargassum seaweed floats near the surface in big clumps, providing food and shelter for fish and crabs.

Plankton

Gannets dive into the water from the air, snapping up fish in their beaks.

Gannets are large seabirds.

Ocean sunfish sunbathe! They float on their sides up near the surface. The sun warms them, then they dive back down to look for food.

Anchovies swim and feed as a group. Working as a team helps them to avoid predators.

Twilight zone

Not much sunlight reaches the **dim** and **murky** twilight zone, but it is still thriving with marine life.

Marine snow

It's raining food!
Marine snow is dead plankton and fish poo that drifts down from the sunlight zone. It is an important source of food for the creatures in the twilight zone.

Instead of hunting, **blobfish** lie in wait, snapping up small crabs and sea urchins who swim too close.

Bristlemouth

TRILLIONS of bristlemouths are thought to live in the twilight zone, making them the BIGGEST GROUP of vertebrates in the world!

Vampire squid feed on marine snow.

Every night, around **5 billion tonnes** (5.5 billion tons) of marine life, such as salps and lanternfish, swim from the depths to the surface of the sea to find food. It's the largest animal migration on Earth.

Lanternfish

Salp

Lanternfish and salps swim up to the sunlight zone during the night. This is to avoid predators who are hunting in the day.

Glass squid can glow. They blend in with the sunlight coming from above, so predators can't see them from below.

Blacksmelt fish have very large eyes that help them search for krill to eat.

Hunters, such as **bluefin tuna**, dive down hundreds of metres from the surface to find prey.

Midnight zone

Beneath the murky twilight zone is the midnight zone. **No sunlight** ever reaches here and it is very cold.

Under pressure

The water from above **presses down** on marine life in the lowest zones. Many creatures here have no bones because they could break from the pressure.

Some animals are used to pressure and need it to hold their shape. **Dumbo octopuses** tend to collapse into a gooey blob if they are brought to the surface.

Being jelly-like helps animals save energy, because instead of swimming, they can just float.

Midnight-zone fish have CHEMICALS in their bodies that help them survive the extreme PRESSURE of the water.

Because it is so dark, **whalefish** rely on a sensitive line on their body to detect prey in the water.

Sensitive line

Bomber worms have glowing sacs, which they drop to distract predators, so that they can escape.

Great swallowers have very stretchy stomachs, so they can eat animals twice their size.

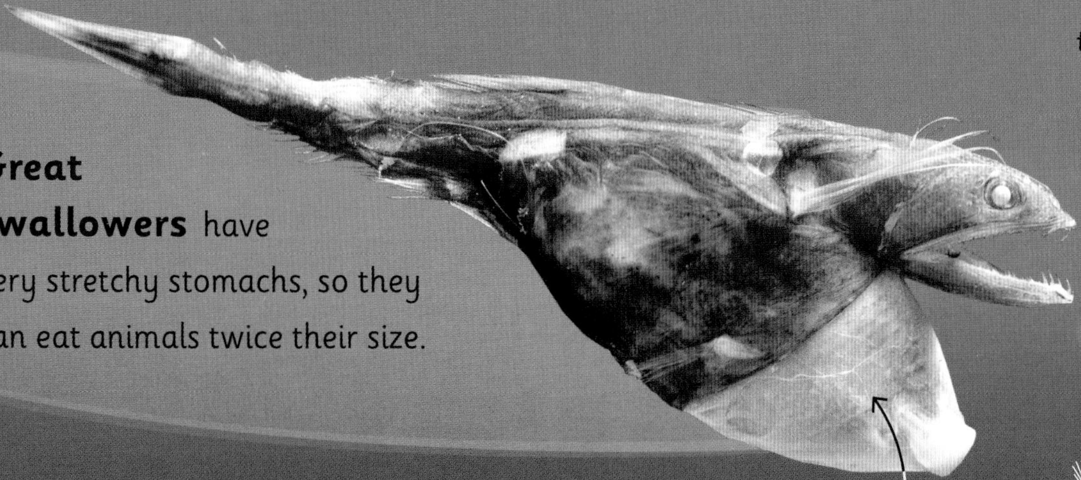

Stretchy stomach

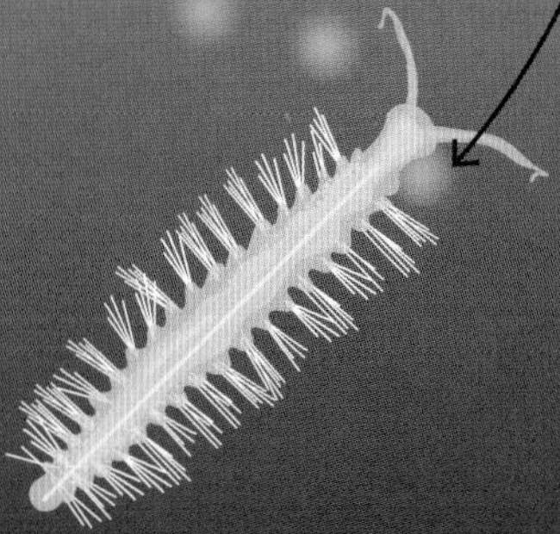

Stoplight loosejaws make their own light. They have glowing spots near their eyes to help them find prey.

Glowing spot

Abyssal zone

It's totally dark, freezing cold, and there's very little food, but some creatures can **survive** in the deepest parts of the ocean.

Fallen feast

Plants cannot grow in the dark, deep sea, so this zone is home to **hunters.** But food is hard to come by so many creatures eat **bacteria**, and the **remains** of whales and fish.

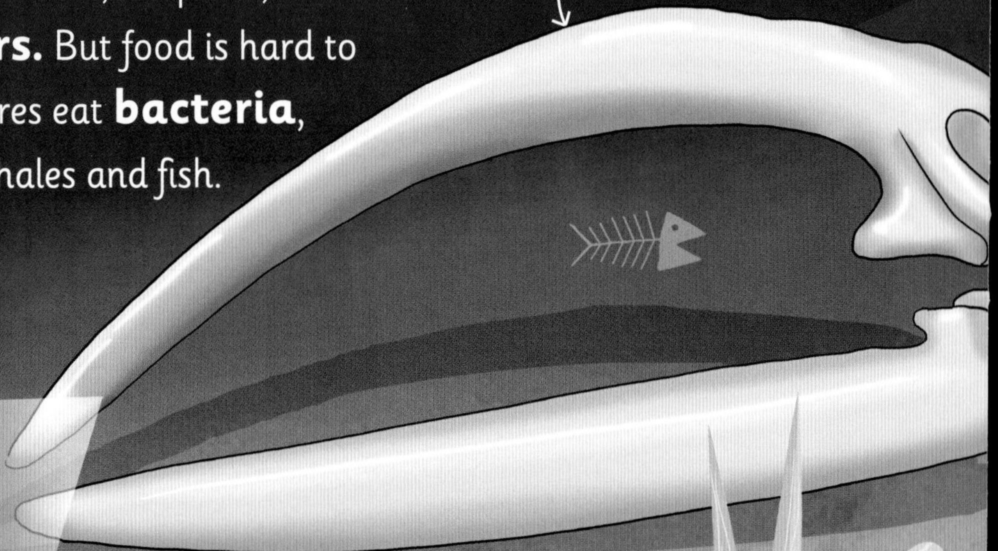

Whale skeleton

Deepwater sea cucumbers slither along the seafloor, swallowing anything they can find to eat.

Bone-eating worm

Bone-eating worms live in and feed off the bones of dead creatures, such as whales.

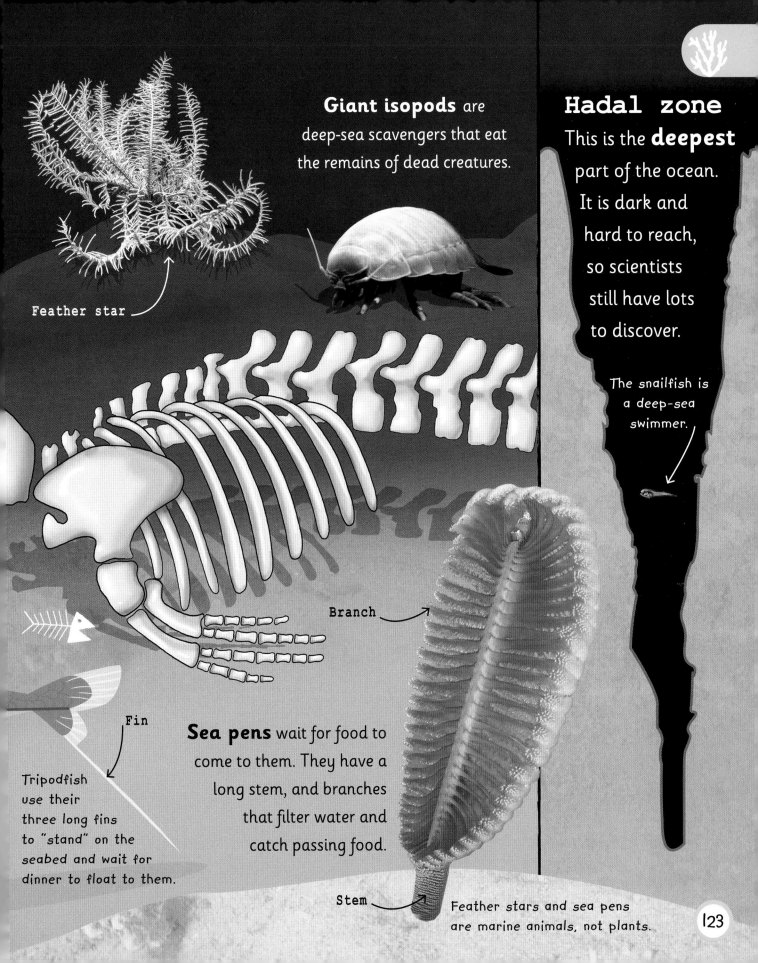

Giant isopods are deep-sea scavengers that eat the remains of dead creatures.

Feather star

Hadal zone

This is the **deepest** part of the ocean. It is dark and hard to reach, so scientists still have lots to discover.

The snailfish is a deep-sea swimmer.

Branch

Fin

Tripodfish use their three long fins to "stand" on the seabed and wait for dinner to float to them.

Sea pens wait for food to come to them. They have a long stem, and branches that filter water and catch passing food.

Stem

Feather stars and sea pens are marine animals, not plants.

Living in the ocean

There are some seriously **skilled creatures** beneath the waves. From clever masters of disguise to cunning prey that take drastic measures to stay alive, the ocean is full of action. So dive in and meet the curious creatures making waves in the water.

Family matters

Ocean families come in all shapes and sizes. Some animals rely on members of their family to survive, while others may never even meet theirs.

Eggs

When a female **cardinal fish** lays her eggs, the male gathers them into his mouth. The male won't eat anything until the eggs have hatched and the babies swim out.

Male **emperor penguins** look after their egg while the female searches for food. She won't come back for two months! The male keeps the egg warm until it hatches. When the female returns, both parents go out to catch food and the chicks huddle together.

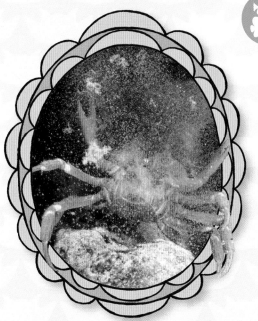

Baby **whales** are called **calves**. They are cared for by their mothers. Grandmother whales share food with their daughter's babies. They all stay with the same family, called a "pod", for their whole lives.

Red crabs may never meet their parents. The mother lays her eggs on the beach, before the hatchlings get washed out to sea.

Eggs

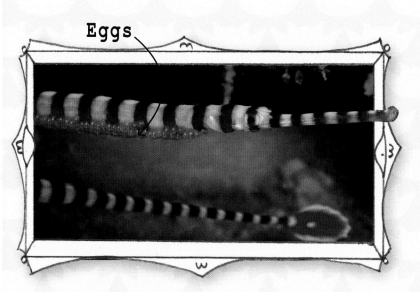

Male **pipefish** keep a row of eggs stuck to their bodies until they hatch. Then the babies drift off and live on their own.

Sea lions live in colonies. A male always stands guard when mothers feed their young.

Turtle power

1

Craaaack! The turtle hatchling breaks free by pecking out of its egg.

Baby turtles do not have the easiest start to life. Their mother lays her eggs on the beach and when they hatch, they must **race to the ocean**. Get set, go!

2

All of these eggs must mean other babies are going to arrive!

Craaack Craaack

The tiny turtle measures about the same length as your thumb. Once hatched, it must travel to its new home – the ocean.

3

The turtle crawls along the sand towards the ocean. It is not far, but every second is risky because the hatchling is slow, and there are predators waiting on the beach.

4

Shadows are a sign of danger so I avoid them!

Hungry seabirds circle the beach and prepare to swoop down from the skies.

5

Eeeek!

The hatchling avoids crabs and other predators until it finally reaches the ocean.

6

In the ocean, the turtle must swim without stopping to escape the sunny, shallow water where it is still in danger from predators, including dolphins. Over time, the turtle will grow bigger and stronger.

7

I hope my babies can make it to the water!

As an adult, the turtle returns to the same beach to lay its eggs. Its hatchlings will experience the same race to the ocean.

Riding
the waves

Many creatures swim the seas, but swimming is not the only **motion** in the ocean! There are all kinds of ways to get around.

Sailfish

Deadly drifter

Beware the **Portuguese man o' war** with its trailing, toxic tentacles. It relies on ocean currents to drift in the water.

Portuguese man o' war

Speedy swimmer

The **sailfish** is smooth, sleek, and streamlined, which helps it zoom through the ocean at turbo speeds. Its long, pointed bill cuts through the water, and its fins help it turn.

The sailfish is the fastest creature in water, reaching speeds of 112 kph (70 mph) – the same speed as a car on a motorway!

Tummy travel

Sea otters carry their young on their tummies as they float along. The pup can feed on its mother's milk as they float.

Sea otters

Jumbo jet

Octopuses squeeze their bodies tightly, causing jets of water to push out and move them along through the water. This is called **jet propulsion**.

Octopus

Hitching a ride

Barnacles don't work too hard! They stick themselves to a boat or turtle and go along for the ride.

Barnacles

Flying machine

Sea turtles use flippers to "fly" underwater — just like birds use their wings to fly through the sky.

Sea turtle

Swimming together

It's tough being a small creature in the big ocean. That's why some animals form special **groups**. Working as a team can keep them safe from predators — it's also a helpful way to hunt.

I'm hungry, but when small fish move in a ball shape, I can't catch them!

Bait ball

School

We all swim in the same direction.

SCHOOLS can contain THOUSANDS of fish!

A frenzy of fish

A **shoal** of fish is less structured than a school. It is a loose cluster of fish that can contain one or many different types, and even other creatures!

I find it harder to catch tiny fish when they work together.

Shoal

Let's confuse these hungry dolphins!

Synchronised swimmers

A **school** of fish is very organised. All of the fish twist, turn, and move as one. Schools of fish are all of the same species.

Pod

These fish are all so organised.

They're beautiful!

Peas in a pod

Some marine mammals, such as dolphins, whales, and seals, live in small groups called **pods**. They hunt for prey together, and protect each other.

Perfect partners

The ocean is full of partnerships. Sea creatures **help** each other out in many ways and some even rely on each other to survive.

Sea anemones and clownfish

Sea anemones let clownfish **hide** from predators among their stinging tentacles. In return, clownfish bring oxygen-rich water, and **clean** the anemone's tentacles for them.

Clownfish

Shlurp!

Lick

Sea anemone

Snapping shrimps and gobies

These partners live together. While the shrimp is making the burrow, the goby will **watch out** for predators.

Thank you for sharing your home with us.

Goby

Snapping shrimp

Coral and algae

Tiny algae **lives inside** coral, out of reach of fish who might eat it. The algae gives the coral its spectacular colours, and also **feeds** on it.

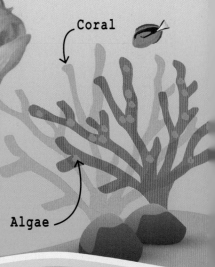

Coral

Algae

Clownfish also ATTRACT PREY

Cleaning creatures

Cleaner fish and shrimp eat the **dead skin** that is on big fish. The big fish gets a clean and the tiny fish get a meal!

I clean blue tangs, parrotfish, and snappers.

Yum!

Yummy!

Barnacles and whales

Boxer crabs and sea anemones

Algae and spider crabs

Barnacles and whales both eat **plankton**. Barnacles cling to the backs and bellies of whales. Then the whales take them to where the plankton can be found.

Boxer crabs carry sea anemones on their claws. They use them like **boxing gloves** to sting predators. In return, the crabs feed the sea anemones.

Algae clings to a spider crab's shell. The algae gets a home, and its green-brown colour **camouflages** the crab.

Algae

Spider crab

Whale

Boxer crab

Anemone

Barnacle

for the sea anemones.

Ocean wanderers

Epic journeys called **migrations** are part of life for some marine creatures. They may travel long distances across vast oceans to feed or breed.

We have a long journey ahead of us!

Eels

Eel babies drift from the Sargasso Sea in the Atlantic Ocean, to Europe, which takes about 300 days. Then, when they become adults, they migrate back again.

I travel from the USA to the North Pacific twice a year in search of food.

Migrating **spiny lobsters** walk in single file along the seabed until they reach warmer waters.

Northern elephant seal

Spiny lobsters

Once a year, **blue marlin** migrate thousands of miles to get to warmer, tropical waters.

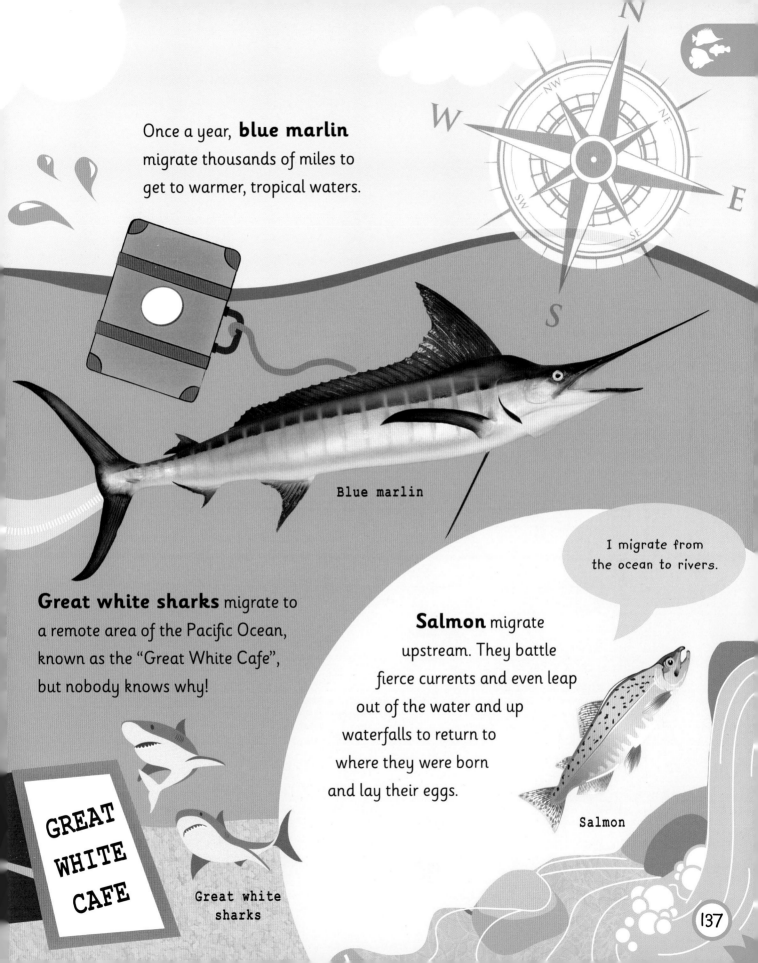

Blue marlin

Great white sharks migrate to a remote area of the Pacific Ocean, known as the "Great White Cafe", but nobody knows why!

GREAT WHITE CAFE

Great white sharks

Salmon migrate upstream. They battle fierce currents and even leap out of the water and up waterfalls to return to where they were born and lay their eggs.

I migrate from the ocean to rivers.

Salmon

Whale
adventure

Every year, **humpback whales** swim thousands of miles from the cold waters of Antarctica to the warmer Pacific, Indian, and Atlantic Oceans.

Humpbacks form a circle and make a "net" of bubbles to trap prey.

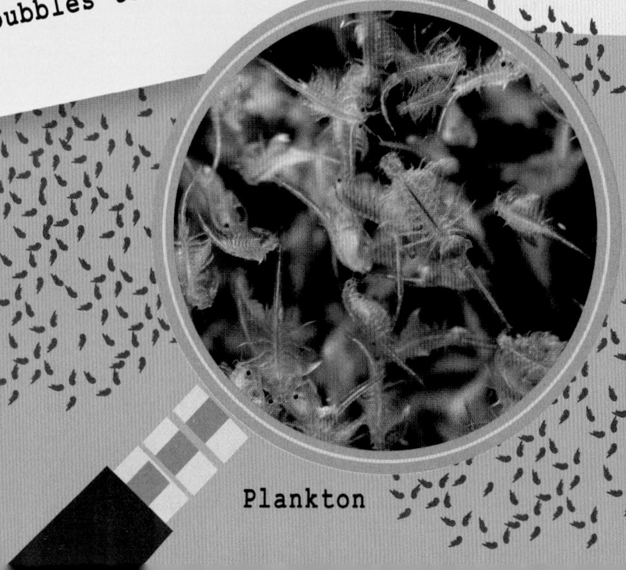

Plankton

HUMPBACK WHALES have one

1 Humpbacks migrate from their **feeding** site to their **breeding** ground. They eat lots of tiny plankton and krill to build body fat before their long journey.

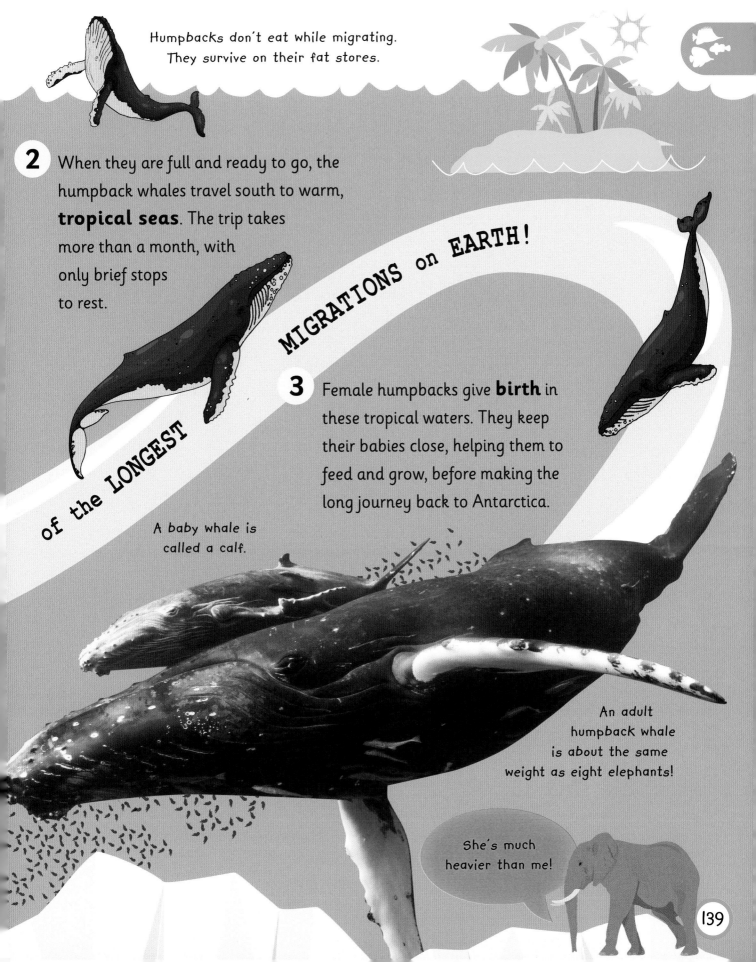

Humpbacks don't eat while migrating. They survive on their fat stores.

2 When they are full and ready to go, the humpback whales travel south to warm, **tropical seas**. The trip takes more than a month, with only brief stops to rest.

of the LONGEST MIGRATIONS on EARTH!

A baby whale is called a calf.

3 Female humpbacks give **birth** in these tropical waters. They keep their babies close, helping them to feed and grow, before making the long journey back to Antarctica.

An adult humpback whale is about the same weight as eight elephants!

She's much heavier than me!

Arctic food web

All animals need food for **energy**, and those that live in the same habitat are linked by a food web.

Arctic char

Pass it on

Starting at the Sun, energy is passed from algae to small animals, then onto predators, who are at the top of the **food web**.

Arctic cod

Small fish, such as Arctic cod, feast on zooplankton. Fish are an important food source for bigger animals.

Phytoplankton

At the start of the food web are tiny phytoplankton. They are essential food for tiny marine life called zooplankton.

Zooplankton

Arctic tern

Polar bear

Ringed seal

Bigger animals, such as seals
and birds, feast on lots of
fish, but are at risk
from predators.

At the top of the food web
are hunters, such as polar
bears and orcas. These top
predators feed on fish, but
also large creatures,
including seals.

Narwhal

Orca

Amazing algae

At the bottom of the ocean food chain are tiny marine algae called **phytoplankton**. They are small, but there are billions of them floating in the ocean.

Phytoplankton are called "the grass of the sea" because so many creatures depend on them.

Phytoplankton float on the surface of the ocean. This helps sunlight reach them.

Phytoplankton produce HALF the

Phytoplankto

Fish food

Phytoplankton are very important. They provide food for all kinds of marine life, including zooplankton and some crustaceans. They are the **largest producers** of food in the ocean and without them, the ocean's food chain would break down.

They are tiny but if you look closely, you might see phytoplankton floating in tide pools at the beach.

Carbon dioxide

Oxygen supply

Phytoplankton use a mixture of sunlight, water, and carbon dioxide to make energy. This process is called **photosynthesis**. As they take in carbon dioxide, they release oxygen into the air, which helps us breathe.

Energy is passed from phytoplankton to the animals that eat them.

Magnified phytoplankton

Oxygen

oxygen we BREATHE!

Big blooms

Phytoplankton can grow very quickly to create **algal blooms**. These cover huge areas and attract lots of hungry sea creatures. But some blooms are toxic and can harm the marine life.

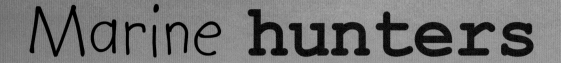

Marine hunters

All marine creatures must **find food** to survive.
Some hunt using their super senses, sharp teeth,
and spectacular speed!

The **shortfin mako shark** is
also known as the "cheetah of
the ocean". It's a seriously fast
mover that can leap out of the
water when chasing prey.

Shortfin mako
shark

We sense vibrations caused by
tiny fish and trap the culprits
with our sharp teeth.

We are slow,
but deadly.

Jellyfish

Ribbon eels

Jellyfish float through the water.
They can paralyse passing prey,
allowing them to dig into dinner
without having to move.

The peacock mantis shrimp is strong enough

Humpback
whales

Humpback whales hunt in groups.
They blow bubbles from their blowhole.
Rising bubbles form a net shape, trapping
fish or krill inside, ready for a family feast.

The ink-squirting **Australian giant
cuttlefish** targets fast-moving prey, such
as fish. This creature waits, before shooting
out its tentacles and striking at speed.

Black ink confuses
predators.

Australian giant
cuttlefish

Peacock mantis
shrimp

The **peacock mantis shrimp** creeps up
on crabs and punches them with its claw. Its
punch has the force of a bullet!

to PUNCH through thick GLASS!

Self defence

Many ocean creatures blend into their surroundings to avoid being attacked, but others have clever ways to **fight**, **trick**, or **confuse** their enemies.

Sting in the tail

The **stingray** has two spikes on its tail that are full of venom. When in danger, it flicks its tail to attack.

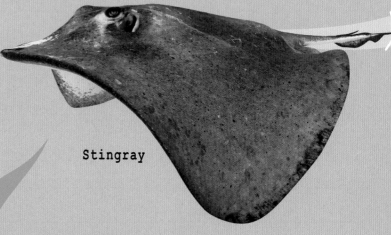

Stingray

Vanishing act

Releasing a cloudy black ink allows the **octopus** to hide from passing predators and swim away without being seen.

The cube boxfish produces toxic mucus when it is stressed.

Octopus

I can produce slime when I am in danger!

Stonefish venom can KILL

I can puff up to three times my usual size!

Normal porcupinefish

Puff power

The **porcupinefish** sucks in water and inflates itself. This makes it bigger and more frightening to larger predators. Its sharp spines also stick out when it's inflated, making it much more difficult to eat!

Porcupinefish fully puffed up

Poisonous spines

Spines warn predators to stay away from the **lionfish**. But if that doesn't scare them, the spines are also highly poisonous.

Lionfish

Stonefish

Very venomous

It look like harmless coral, but the **stonefish** has small spines on its fins that can inject a deadly venom.

a human within an HOUR.

Masters of disguise

Ocean survival can be tricky, so many creatures are experts at hiding. They can match their homes, mimic other animals, or transform to **blend in** with their surroundings.

Camouflage king

Cuttlefish can change their colour, shape, or texture to look like different habitats, such as the seabed or coral. This is called **camouflage**.

Sea urchins create a new look by picking up shells and stones off the ocean floor.

I'm pretending to be seaweed.

Who do I look like?

The **mimic octopus** sits on the seabed and impersonates poisonous animals, such as starfish and sea snakes.

Leafy sea dragons have green, floaty frills, which allow them to hide in seagrass and seaweed.

Cuttlefish have millions of skin cells that change colour in less than a second.

Can you *see* me, or coral?

The stripes of the **lionfish** break up the outline of its body, making it harder to see from far away.

I'm almost invisible!

Little crustaceans called **hyperiid amphipods** have see-through bodies, so they look almost invisible to predators.

Natural **glow**

Some living things create their own light, called **bioluminescence**. These marine creatures make the ocean look like it is filled with bright, shining stars.

Why do animals glow?

Creatures use their natural glow to scare and confuse predators, trick prey, attract mates, and blend in with sun-soaked water.

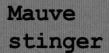

Shining lights

Let's meet a few of the **thousands of creatures** shining a light on the oceans.

Anglerfish

In the deep, dark sea, the anglerfish makes its own light to attract prey. This light **swings** from its head.

Mauve stinger

When waves move this jellyfish, it glows. If touched by another creature, the mauve stinger releases a shiny, **sticky spew**!

Whoosh!

Electric blue

Vaadhoo Island, in the Maldives, is a paradise island that becomes even more beautiful at night. The crashing waves make marine algae, called **phytoplankton**, light up electric blue.

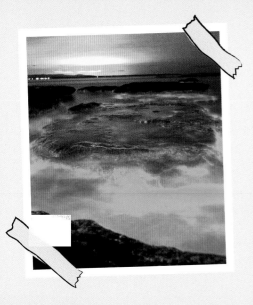

Phytoplankton

Comb jelly

The body of the comb jelly is almost entirely **see-through**, but its bioluminescence brightens the dark water.

Hatchetfish

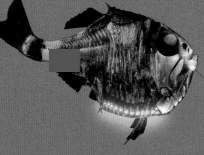

The hatchetfish has **lights** on its belly which hide its dark shadow. Enemies dismiss the light as a glow from the ocean surface.

Flashlight fish

The flashlight fish gets its name from the **glowing organs** under its eyes. It lives in coral reefs, and is one of the few shallow-water fish that produce light.

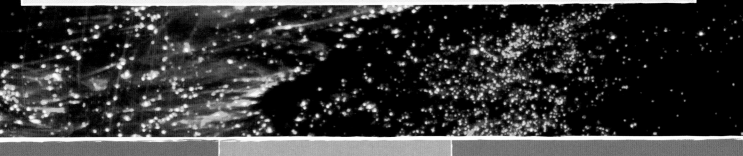

Sea of **sounds**

The sea can be a noisy place. Making and listening to sounds helps animals to **communicate**, **search** for food, and **find** their way.

Bark!

Male **California sea lions** bark to scare off other males and to defend their homes.

Bark!

Bark!

Pop!

Clownfish make popping and chirping noises to show off to other clownfish, and to make themselves seem scarier than they are.

POP!

Snap!

Pistol shrimp snap an enlarged claw to make a stream of exploding bubbles, which stun their prey. The noise can be louder than a firework!

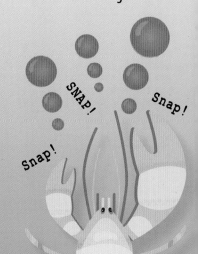

SNAP!

Snap!

Snap!

CLOWNFISH make some of their

I sometimes slap my tail to get my friends' attention.

SPLASH!

Splish!

Dolphins slap their tail onto the surface of the ocean. The loud splash startles fish, making them scurry out of their hiding places.

Hoot!

Woof!
Squawk!

Male **oyster toadfish** build their nests out of shells and rocks. They then make low hooting sounds to attract mates.

HOOT!
HOOT!

When **swellsharks** are threatened, they suck in water and inflate to twice their size. Once the danger passes, they release the water and make a barking sound – just like a dog!

WOOF!

Batfish sing at dawn and dusk. Their squawks, burbles, and pops mix with the sounds of other fish to create an underwater chorus!

Burble!

Pop!

Squawk!

sounds using their TEETH!

Super sonar

Imagine how difficult it would be to swim in the dark! Dolphins use a special **sonar system**, where sound helps them "see" underwater.

click click

1 When the Sun or Moon are hidden, the ocean can get dark. This makes it hard for a dolphin to get around or find **food**.

2 Rather than using its sight to navigate through the water, a dolphin will use its **sonar**. It will make clear, clicking sounds.

There's a thick pad, or "melon" in my forehead. This helps me produce clicking sounds. I can make up to 1,000 clicks every second!

3 These clicks travel as **sound waves** through the water around the dolphin. Sound waves travel almost five times faster in water than in air!

click click click click

Listening to the echoes helps me work out the size, shape, and location of prey. I think I've found an octopus!

Most dolphin clicks are too high-pitched for humans to hear.

ck

4 The sound waves travel until they hit something, such as prey. The waves then **bounce off** the prey and travel straight back to the dolphin as echoes.

click

5 The longer it takes for the echoes to return, the bigger the distance between the dolphin and prey. This sonar system is called **echolocation**.

Dolphins can hear TWICE as well as CATS!

Smart sea creatures

From super-smart whales to problem-solving octopuses, there are some big **brainboxes** under the sea.

whistle... click... whistle...

whistle... click...

Sperm whale

Orca

Brainy beast

A whale's brain is **highly developed**, allowing it to communicate, solve puzzles, and even recognize itself. A sperm whale's brain is the largest of any mammal on Earth.

Clever communicator

Adult orcas and other dolphins "speak" to each other in clicks and whistles. They pass on **information**, such as where to find food, including seals.

I don't want to be supper!

Problem solver

An octopus has a big brain, and **nerve cells** in its arms, which control movement. It is good at solving problems — just like us!

Octopus

Inky's great escape

In 2016, Inky the octopus used his brilliant brain to break out of the National Aquarium in New Zealand.

One evening, Inky noticed that the lid to his tank was slightly open.

He squeezed his flexible body through the gap and crawled along the floor.

He slid down a drainpipe, which led to the ocean. Nobody noticed that Inky had escaped until they spotted a wet trail along the aquarium floor!

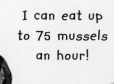

I can eat up to 75 mussels an hour!

Sea otter

Top tool user

The sea otter eats creatures protected by a hard shell, so it must use **tools** to open them. It hammers the shells against rocks to get to the food inside!

Ocean

adventures

People have been **exploring the oceans** for centuries, but now it's your turn to hit the high seas! Get ready for incredible ocean heroes, legendary sea monsters, spectacular shipwrecks, and swashbuckling pirates. What treasures will you uncover?

Early exploration

The oceans have fascinated people since **ancient times**. As people began to sail the seas, their adventures would show our world as never before.

Egyptians

From the 15th century BCE, the Ancient Egyptians sailed south from the Red Sea to **explore** and **trade** with east Africa.

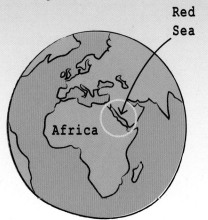

Red Sea

Africa

Heave! Ho!

Phoenicians

These super-sailors used **cedar trees** to make wooden ships. In about 600 BCE, they navigated the coast of Africa.

Cedar tree

Greeks

In around 300 BCE, the Ancient Greeks sailed the Mediterranean Sea and Black Sea, selling goods and **building cities** along the way.

Where shall we go next?

It took the vikings SEVEN DAYS to sail from Scandinavi

Setting sail

The first sailing ships were **wooden**, with a **single sail**. There were oars on board, so the crew could row if there was not enough wind.

Oars

Let's sail the seas!

Vikings

By the 8th century CE, the Vikings of Scandinavia were sailing around Europe and beyond. They sailed to **Iceland** and **Greenland** – lands unknown to Europeans.

Leif Erikson

Viking Leif Erikson and his crew are thought to be the first Europeans to reach North America.

ICELAND.

Polynesians

In the 11th century, the ancient Polynesians searched the Pacific Ocean for **new islands**. They set up homes far and wide, from Hawaii to New Zealand.

Ancient Polynesians relied on the Sun and the stars to find their way.

Polynesian canoe

Silk Road
of the sea

The Silk Road became a **trade route** from the 2nd century BCE. It began in China and continued over land and sea to Europe and Africa.

The overland Silk Road route is in green.

Europe

Asia

Alexandria

Persia

Red Sea

Arabia

Ir

Indian Ocean

Zheng He

Ocean trade

The Silk Road was named after the silk traded by the Chinese. It wasn't just materials that were shared, but also **cultures** and **customs**.

Many TOWNS and temples are

Mapping the Silk Road

The part of the route that went over the sea started in **Guangzhou** in China and went all the way to **Alexandria** in Egypt.

Chinese exploration

By the 15th century, Chinese explorers were setting sail to visit **distant lands** and share goods.

Fantastic fleet

The most famous Chinese captain was Admiral **Zheng He**. Between 1405 and 1433, he led a fleet of 300 ships on seven voyages across the ocean.

Guangzhou

The route over the sea is in blue.

Chinese crew members sent messages between ships using bells, flags, lanterns, and carrier pigeons!

Zheng He used the Chinese invention of the magnetic compass to navigate at sea.

Zheng He traded Chinese silk and Ming vases and in return, he filled his ships with gifts, including pearls, spices, and **exotic animals**.

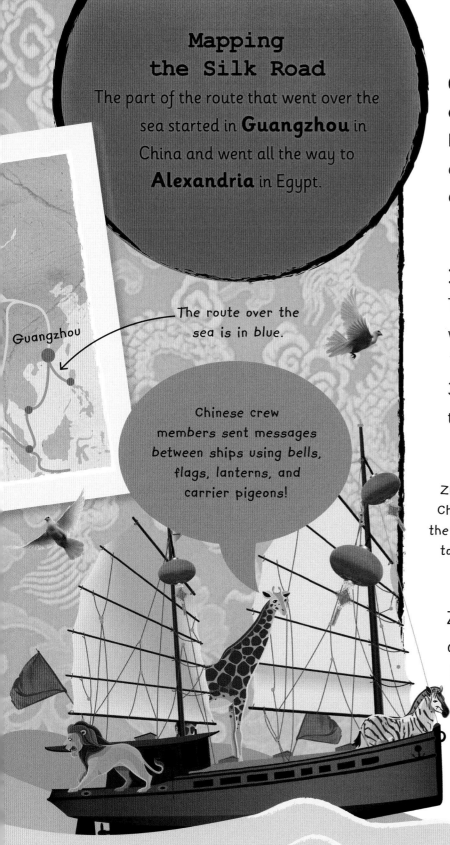

Ocean exploration

The **golden age** of exploration began in the 15th century, when sailors were discovering new routes and reaching distant lands.

Prince Henry of Portugal was given command of some ships in 1415. He used them to explore the coast of **Africa**.

In 1488, Bartolomeu Dias became the first European to sail around the **Cape of Good Hope**, in Africa.

In 1492, Christopher Columbus sailed to the **Caribbean Islands**. He thought this was Asia, but it was actually the Americas!

In the 16th century, Hernán Cortés travelled to Mexico to steal gold from the Aztecs, while Francisco Pizarro sailed to Peru and **seized riches** from the Incas.

European explorers were looking for land in the Pacific Ocean. Captain James Cook arrived in **Australia** in 1770.

Half of my crew died on the voyage to India.

Fallen empires

European explorers brought **problems** for **local people**. They caused fights, stole treasures, and spread diseases. Empires were destroyed and populations wiped out.

Attack of Vasco da Gama's ships.

The first ocean voyage from **Europe to India** was by Portuguese sailor Vasco da Gama, in 1498. He returned with Indian spices.

In 1519, Portuguese explorer, Ferdinand Magellan, led the first trip all the way **around the world**. The voyage proved that the Earth is round.

From 1801 to 1803, English explorer Matthew Flinders sailed all the way around **Australia**.

European traders wanted a route east, but due to the icy coast of Siberian Russia, the **Northeast Passage** wasn't fully navigated until 1878.

Rather than sailing the stormy seas around North America, explorers tried travelling northwest to Asia. The **Northwest Passage** was finally sailed in 1906.

Science at sea

For years, scientists have researched the sea and travelled to exotic places in search of **new species**. Their findings have helped us learn much more about the natural world.

Aristotle

Zoology is the study of animals.

Ancient discoveries

In the 4th century BCE, Greek philosopher Aristotle studied different animals and divided them into groups. He was the first person to sort nature in this way, and his work is considered the beginning of **zoology**.

Watery work

German scientist Alexander von Humboldt sailed to South America in 1799. He gathered lots of wildlife, and studied **ocean currents** and **weather patterns**. He discovered so much that his findings filled 34 huge books!

Alexander von Humboldt

Famous fossil finder

In 1811, British schoolgirl Mary Anning found a skeleton on her local beach. It turned out to be an ichthyosaur – a **prehistoric** marine reptile! She discovered hundreds more fossils in her lifetime, which helped scientists to build a better picture of our ancient oceans.

Mary Anning

Ichthyosaur fossil

HMS Beagle

Many people didn't trust Mary's findings and some even took credit for her work.

Beaky birds

In 1831, naturalist Charles Darwin left England, UK, and sailed the globe on board *HMS Beagle*. He studied wildlife, and found animals were slightly different on each of the Galápagos Islands in South America – they had **adapted** to suit their local environment.

Medium ground finch

Vegetarian finch

Woodpecker finch

Green warbler finch

Darwin found 18 species of finches, each with different shaped beaks.

167

Ships ahoy!

Over the years, boats have become bigger and better. Come aboard some spectacular ships and experience some of the most **memorable journeys** in sailing history.

Ancient canoes

Thousands of years ago, the Polynesians built big, open, **wooden canoes**. They sailed incredible distances across the Pacific Ocean.

On my trip, I seized a ship and stole six tonnes of treasure!

Mayflower

In 1620, this famous ship carried 102 religious people, called **Pilgrims**, on a dangerous voyage from England to North America, to start new lives.

Golden Hind

The *Golden Hind* was sailed by English captain **Sir Francis Drake**. It is remembered for its record-breaking journey around the world, from 1577 to 1580.

SS Normandie

This French ocean liner was the **largest** and **fastest** passenger ship when it launched in 1932. It was very luxurious and even had a winter garden on board.

U.S.S. Constitution

Launched in 1797, the *Constitution* is the oldest commissioned ship in the US Navy. It was nicknamed "**Old Ironsides**", because cannons couldn't defeat it.

The World

With 165 permanent homes, this is the world's biggest **private residential ship**. Since its launch in 2002, *The World* has travelled the globe.

Searching for shipwrecks

Not all ships are sailing along the ocean's surface. Beneath the waves you will find **millions of ships** resting on rocks and scattered along the ocean floor. These are the world's shipwrecks.

Deep-sea discoveries

Underwater explorers have found many shipwrecks and uncovered **fascinating relics** from the past...

Buried treasure

The ***Queen Anne's Revenge*** belonged to 18th century pirate Blackbeard. He captured the ship, and filled it with cannons and a bloodthirsty crew. Plenty of pirate plunder was later discovered aboard the sunken shipwreck.

Why do boats sink?

Ships sink for many reasons. Some are struck by **storms** and high seas. Others **capsize** or are crushed in collisions. Many ships simply **leak**, fill with water, and sink.

Shipwrecks can contain treasure and secrets about the past. But many remain undiscovered, their whereabouts a mystery.

Remarkable relics

More than 80,000 pieces of porcelain and treasure were uncovered from the wreck of 13th-century Chinese merchant ship **Nanhai One**. These relics give an insight into the history of Chinese trade.

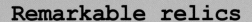

Frozen in time

In 1912, just four days into her first voyage, **Titanic** struck an iceberg and sank. It took 73 years to find the wreck, but when they did, divers rescued many items, including a pocket watch stuck at the time the ship sank.

Before setting sail, *Titanic* was said to be "unsinkable".

Terrors of the sea

Many years ago, sailors had to watch out for treasure-hungry criminals looking to steal their cargo – **beware of the pirates**!

Don't leave me here!

Life at sea

Pirates of the past endured crowded, **rat-infested ships** for months at a time. Their captain would set strict rules to control the crew and to keep the boat shipshape.

If a pirate broke the rules, they would be left on a desert island as punishment.

Parrot

Pirates would trap **PARROTS** and sell them for lots of **MONEY**!

The Jolly Roger is the most famous pirate flag in history. It was designed to scare anyone who saw it.

I'm one of the most famous and fearsome pirates in history.

Blackbeard

King of the pirates

Pirates wanted to be feared. Eighteenth-century English pirate, **Blackbeard**, was cruel and bad-tempered. He would light fuses in his beard to scare people. The hissing strings made him look like a monster.

Ching Shih

Powerful pirate queen

Nineteenth-century Chinese pirate **Ching Shih** was the fearsome commander of nearly 2,000 ships and up to 70,000 pirates. She was a strict leader who often defeated the government. Ching Shih would severely punish any pirate who dared to break her rules.

Myths and legends

For centuries, people have **shared stories** of sea monsters and lost cities. Let's take a look at some of these tall tales.

Mermaids

Mermaids are said to have the head and body of a woman but the **tail of a fish**. Some say they bring sailors safety at sea, while others believe they are a warning of storms.

Explorer Christopher Columbus is thought to have mistaken manatees for mermaids!

Umibôzu

This **Japanese sea spirit** is thought to rise from calm waters during the night, and attack ships. This spirit is named "sea monk" after its bald head, and some say it is the ghost of a drowned priest.

Kraken

A huge sea monster, called the Kraken, is said to lurk in the waters off Norway and Greenland, waiting to **pull ships** to their doom.

Atlantis

According to legend, the ancient city of Atlantis **sank beneath the waves**, destroying an entire civilization. Today, scientists are using the latest technology to look for lost cities like this one.

Sirens

These dangerous women, from Greek mythology, would sing enchanting melodies to **lure sailors** closer. Then the sirens would sink the ships and drown the sailors.

Exploring machines

Submarines and submersibles travel **deep underwater** and explore the ocean. These marvellous machines are designed to cope with extreme water pressure in the sea.

Submarines

These **huge machines** carry the navy deep below the ocean's surface. They have enough power and space for the crew to stay underwater for months.

Submersibles

These underwater machines are much **smaller** and **less powerful** than submarines. They are launched from ships to explore and carry out research.

Alvin

This super-submersible launched in 1964 and has made about 5,000 dives. The scientists aboard Alvin discovered hydrothermal vents.

How submarines work

When the tanks on a submarine are **filled** with water, it becomes heavy and sinks. To come back up, water is **forced out** of the tanks to make the submarine lighter.

Shinkai 6500

This submersible can reach incredible depths, allowing scientists to carry out deep-sea research and predict earthquakes.

How submersibles work

Submersibles work in a similar way to submarines, but most are **controlled remotely** by people on ships at the ocean's surface. Only a few submersibles carry people.

DSRV

If a submarine sinks, emergency Deep Sea Rescue Vehicles (DSRV) are sent to help crews trapped on board and bring them safely to the surface.

Air is forced out.

Air is blown in.

Tank releases water to rise.

Tank hovers underwater.

Tank fills with water to sink.

Nautilus

The world's first nuclear-powered submarine was *Nautilus*, which launched in 1954. It was the first vessel to reach the North Pole.

DeepFlight

These small submarines are used for fun. They can "fly" through the water at high speeds.

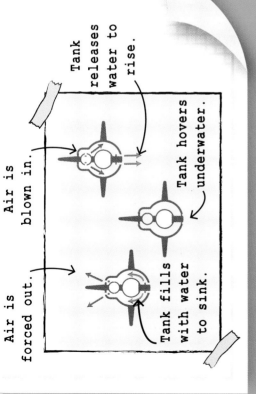

Ocean equipment

From the shallow surface to the deepest, darkest depths, technology wizards have **invented** all kinds of amazing equipment to help us explore the world's waters.

Snorkel

This simple **mask** and **breathing tube** helps people to swim underwater at shallow depths and see the marine life clearly.

Snorkel

Buoys are fixed floats that mark out points in the sea, such as safe swimming areas. They can also monitor the weather and waves.

Scuba-diving kit

Scuba equipment allows divers to **explore the deep** ocean. An air-filled cylinder helps divers to breathe, and a mask allows them to see underwater. They also use fins to help them swim.

Air-filled cylinder

Mask

Fins

Scuba diver

Satellites

Circling above Earth are satellites. Sailors use equipment to detect signals from satellites, which help guide their boat safely through the ocean.

Lighthouse **LIGHTS** can be seen from **MANY MILES** away.

Lighthouse light

Lighthouses

Lighthouses have been guiding sailors for years. The bright beacons on top of these tall towers **warn ships** of choppy seas or rocky coastlines.

Hydrophones

Special underwater **microphones**, called "hydrophones", can detect sounds and play them back. These devices can pick up whale songs!

Hydrophone

Scientists stay safely above water while remotely operated vehicles (ROVs) carry out deep-sea research without anyone on board.

Ewwwweyyyoooo

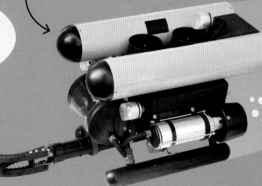

Mapping the ocean

As technology improves, scientists use it to find out more about the ocean, and make **detailed maps** of the ocean floor.

Marine mission

In 1872, *HMS Challenger*, a British research ship, set off to **learn more** about the ocean. It was a floating science laboratory, with bottles to collect water samples and nets to gather creatures.

HMS Challenger

In 1882, the *Albatross*, set sail from the USA. It was the first ship built by any government for oceanographic research.

The laboratory on board *HMS Challenger*.

HMS Challenger's journey was the start of modern oceanography – the study of oceans.

A specimen from the original research

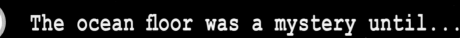

Sonar image of the ocean floor off California, USA.

Research ship

Huge efforts are being made to map the seabed in greater detail.

Superb sonar

By the 20th century, scientists were using sonar technology to work out the **depth of the ocean**, and to find objects under the surface of the ocean.

A ship uses sonar to send sound waves down to the seabed.

The time it takes for sound waves to return to the ship is used to work out the distance to the seabed.

In the mid-20th century, Americans Marie Tharp and Bruce Heezen made the first detailed map of the ocean floor.

Most of the ocean floor still needs to be mapped by sonar!

There's still a lot to discover!

Deep discoveries

Since the 19th century, scientists have been going **deeper** to explore the oceans. They have uncovered some extraordinary things.

1840

Sir James Clark Ross, nephew of Sir John Ross, measured the depth of the ocean using a weighted rope.

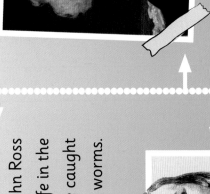

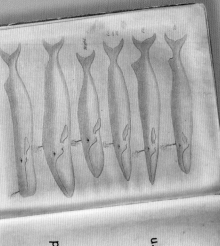

1855

American sailor Matthew Maury found that ships can travel faster using ocean winds and currents. He also wrote the first book of modern oceanography.

1818

Scottish explorer Sir John Ross realised there was life in the deep sea when he caught starfish and worms.

1841

Naturalist Edward Forbes explored the Mediterranean. He thought that nothing lived deeper than 548 m (1,800 ft), but was proved wrong!

Basket star

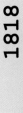

1857

The first submarine valley was discovered at Monterey Canyon, California. American officer James Alden revealed the hollow in the seabed.

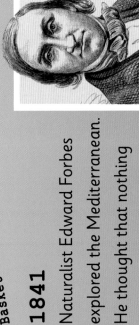

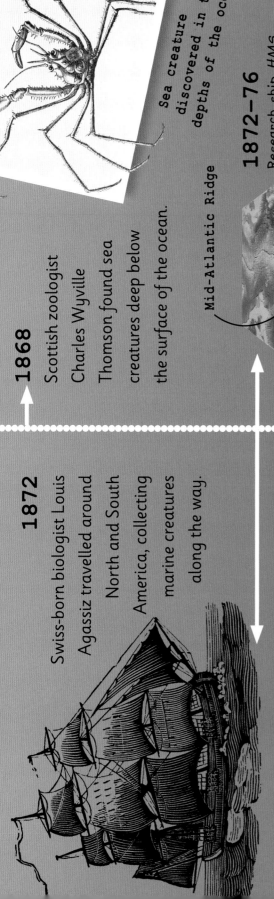

1868

Scottish zoologist Charles Wyville Thomson found sea creatures deep below the surface of the ocean.

Sea creature discovered in the depths of the ocean.

1872–76

Research ship HMS Challenger discovered mountains, trenches, and the Mid-Atlantic Ridge – the world's longest underwater mountain chain.

Mid-Atlantic Ridge

1930

American explorers William Beebe and Otis Barton went deeper into the ocean than ever before. They travelled in their steel submersible and spotted different deep-sea life, including glowing jellyfish!

1872

Swiss-born biologist Louis Agassiz travelled around North and South America, collecting marine creatures along the way.

1898

German biologist Carl Chun sailed the subantarctic seas and discovered the vampire squid.

1925–27

A German meteor expedition resulted in the first detailed survey of the south Atlantic Ocean.

Exploring the
Mariana Trench

With icy temperatures and crushing pressure, only a few people have explored the **deepest point** on Earth.

If you DROPPED A ROCK into the Mariana Trench, it would take more than AN HOUR to reach the bottom!

Mariana Trench

This trench is 11,034 m (36,200 ft) deep and lies between Japan and Australia in the **Pacific Ocean.** It is so deep that if Mount Everest (the highest point on Earth) stood in the trench, its peak would be completely underwater!

Deep down

Underwater trenches are formed where two pieces of the **Earth's crust** collide and are pushed down.

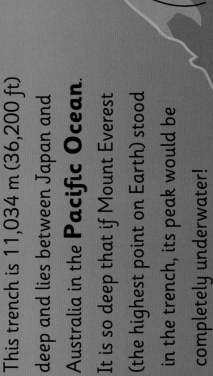

The crust comes together and forms a V-shaped trench.

Mount Everest's peak is 8,848 m (29,029 ft) above ground.

American explorer Victor Vescovo is the first person to visit the top of Mount Everest and the bottom of the Mariana Trench.

There have been very few **expeditions** to the depths of the Mariana Trench...

Historic journey

In 1960, **Jacques Piccard** and **Don Walsh** became the first people to visit the Mariana Trench. They travelled in a submersible called *Trieste* and it took five hours to reach the bottom.

Jacques Piccard

> We saw an unknown sea creature, proving there was life in the deep.

Trieste

Solo trip

In 2012, film director **James Cameron** made the deepest solo dive in history. He travelled in a submarine called *Deepsea Challenger*, which took two and a half hours to reach the deepest point on Earth.

Deepsea Challenger

James Cameron took photos and collected samples from the bottom of the trench.

Third time lucky

In 2019, **Victor Vescovo** travelled to the depths of the Mariana Trench in a submersible called *Limiting Factor*. He went deeper than anyone had before, and discovered creatures including shrimp-like amphipods and spoon worms. He has been back several times since 2019.

Amphipod

Spoon worm

Limiting Factor

A plastic bag at the bottom showed the extent of plastic pollution.

Underwater mountains

Lots of mountains lie beneath the ocean. These **seamounts** create a healthy habitat for marine life.

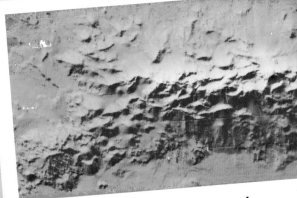

The tallest seamounts can be detected by satellites. Smaller ones are harder to spot and can only be found using sonar.

What is a seamount?

Seamounts are **underwater mountains** that rise from the seafloor. They are big, but do not break through the surface of the water.

Ocean currents

The exact number of seamounts is unknown.

Ocean currents swirl around seamounts and bring nutrients for marine life to eat.

Seamounts provide a useful landmark for migrating sea animals.

Most seamounts are EXTINCT VOLCANOES, so they

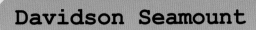

Davidson Seamount

A super-sized seamount lies off the coast of **California, USA**. The Davidson Seamount measures 2,279 m (7,480 ft) tall, but its peak remains below the surface.

In 2002 and 2006, expeditions revealed more about life in the Davidson Seamount.

Life story

The Davidson Seamount is an extinct volcano that last erupted nearly **10 million years ago**. The volcano was first discovered in 1933.

Experts found beautiful coral gardens and 27 types of deep-sea coral, including bubblegum coral.

Remote-operated machines collected coral and rock samples for scientific research.

Seamounts are great to explore!

Bubblegum coral in the Davidson Seamount can grow to over 2.5 m (8 ft) tall!

Bubblegum coral looks like chewed gum!

will NOT ERUPT!

Inside a sinkhole

All across the world's oceans there are large, deep, round, underwater pits called **marine sinkholes**.

The Great Blue Hole

The deepest marine sinkhole is Dragon Hole in the South China Sea. It is as deep as a skyscraper is tall!

What is a marine sinkhole?

A marine sinkhole starts as a **cave** on land. Over time, the ocean rises and the cave sinks underwater. Eventually, the roof of the cave collapses, leaving a **deep pit** full of water.

Super-sized sinkhole

The world's largest sinkhole is the **Great Blue Hole**, in the Caribbean. It attracts divers from all over the world. In 2018, scientists explored its depths.

The Great Blue Hole

Coral

Sea turtle

At first the crew found lots of **marine life**, including coral, sea turtles, and sharks.

Shark

Going deeper, scientists discovered a layer of water that was filled with **dangerous chemicals**. This is natural and can happen when fresh water meets salt water.

Below this layer, no living marine life was found. The chemicals were so **poisonous** that only bacteria could live here.

At the bottom, they found shells, bones, and even a fizzy drinks bottle.

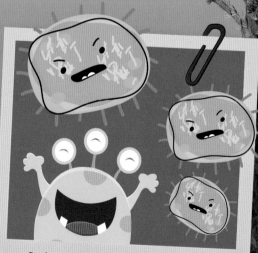

Scientists study how the bacteria at the bottom of sinkholes survives.

189

Ocean heroes

Some **brave** and **brilliant** people have made a splash in the ocean. Let's meet them!

American adventurer **Kathryn Sullivan** was not only the first woman to walk in space, but also to reach the Mariana Trench – the deepest part of the ocean!

German engineer **Erika Bergman** is a submersible pilot who has made hundreds of trips into the deep sea. She also designs ships, submarines, and submersibles.

Cypriot scientist **Ruth Gates** spent her life fighting to save coral reefs. She found a way for special corals to survive the effects of climate change.

Robert Ballard

American oceanographer **Robert Ballard** used submersibles to investigate shipwrecks. He discovered RMS Titanic, the famous cruise ship that hit an iceberg and sank in 1912.

RMS Titanic shipwreck

Indian marine biologist **Suneha Jagannathan** works to restore marine habitats across the world and protect the animals that live there, such as turtles and alligators.

Alligator

In 1888, **Fridtjof Nansen** became the first person to cross the ice of Greenland on skis. This Norwegian explorer discovered new information about glaciers, currents, and climate.

In the 19th century, British botanist **Anna Atkins** created the first printed book with photographs. She used light techniques to make incredible pictures of seaweed.

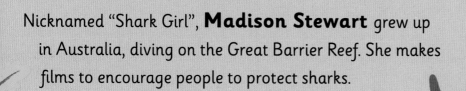

Nicknamed "Shark Girl", **Madison Stewart** grew up in Australia, diving on the Great Barrier Reef. She makes films to encourage people to protect sharks.

Sporting records

Some of the greatest **sporting achievements** have taken place in our oceans.

Join the party!

A **polar bear plunge** is where a group of people run into extremely cold ocean water. The biggest plunge was in Mielno, Poland, when 1,799 people took part!

Deep dive

The deepest scuba dive was by **Ahmed Gabr**. He plunged over 332 m (1,090 ft) into the Red Sea.

It took 12 minutes to go down, but 15 hours to come up!

Brrrrrrrrr!

Wearing just goggles, a swim cap, and swimming trunks, **Lewis Pugh** became the first person to swim beneath the melting Antarctic ice sheet. When he finished, his fingers were almost frozen stiff!

A long swim

Veljko Rogošić, swam almost 140 miles (255 km) across the Adriatic Sea. It took him over two days and is the longest distance ever swum without fins.

Free dive

The women's world record for freediving was set by **Alenka Artnik**, after she dived 114 m (374 ft) in the Red Sea, near Egypt. She did this with no breathing equipment.

Speedy sailing

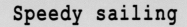

Dame Ellen MacArthur sailed non-stop around the world in only 71 days – and she did it on her own!

A birthday at sea

Maxim Ivanov turned 17 at sea, as he became the youngest person to row across the Atlantic Ocean. The trip was from Portugal to Barbados and took 105 days.

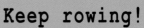

Rowing record

In 2019, four women from Antigua and Barbuda made history as the first **all-Black team** to row across the Atlantic Ocean.

Surf's up!

Maya Gabeira set the record for the largest wave surfed by a female. It was over 22 m (72 ft) high – the height of four giraffes!

Keep rowing!

Roz Savage was the first woman to row across the Atlantic, Pacific, and Indian Oceans. She spent over 500 days alone at sea.

Oceans and us

Oceans are giant playgrounds for beach holidays, thrilling watersports, and scenic boat trips! They are also important sources of food and energy. But human actions can bring problems, so it's up to us to **protect** our incredible oceans for the future.

Fun at sea

The ocean is enormous, leaving a lot of space to go out and **have fun!**

What kind of ocean **activity** do you like best?

Boats are used for all kinds of ocean fun. Large cruise ships are great for relaxing holidays, while smaller sailing boats can be used for races.

Dinghy sailing

Hawaii, Australia, and California are some of the best places to go surfing.

Surfing

Swimming is a fun seaside activity, but be careful not to swim or float too far from the shore.

Swimming

Lots of sea sports require **boards.** They look similar, but boards are all a little different. A paddleboard is flat for a smooth ride, whereas a windsurfing board has a sail to catch the wind.

Paddleboarding

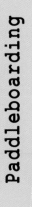

Windsurfing

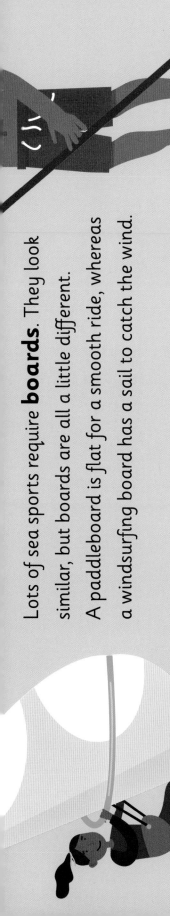

Snorkelling

I use a tube to breathe underwater, but scuba divers use a tank of air.

Scuba diving

Snorkelling and **scuba diving** allow you to get a closer look at marine life. Snorkellers stay close to the water's surface, while scuba divers go deeper.

You need to pass a **TEST** to be able to **SCUBA DIVE.**

Beach holidays

Millions of people flock to beaches around the world to enjoy the Sun, sand, and sea. Grab your swimmers and some sun lotion – we're off to the beach!

Boatloads of tourists flock to this tiny cove found on the Greek island of **Zakynthos**. A shipwreck lies on the sand, while the rocky backdrop looks like a giant crocodile sleeping in the Sun.

The **Maldives** is a chain of paradise islands in the Indian Ocean. With clear, tropical water and incredible marine life, they are popular scuba diving sites.

Zakynthos

Maldives

Copacabana beach

Next to **Miami Beach**, in Florida, USA are promenades, where people roll along on bikes, boards, and rollerblades.

Miami Beach

The swaying palm trees and vast, white sands of **Copacabana beach** in Rio de Janeiro, Brazil, are what make it so popular.

Surfers love catching waves at world-famous **Bondi Beach** in Sydney, Australia. This beach has everything, including fun-filled festivals all year round.

Boulders Beach

Bondi Beach

There is more than just soft sand at **Boulders Beach** in Cape Town, South Africa. A colony of African penguins lives there!

Living underwater

Scientists and explorers

love the idea of living in the ocean. But have any of their designs worked? Jump in to find out...

Underwater habitats

Underwater habitats are **permanent places** below the water's surface, where people can live for weeks at a time. They have areas for eating, working, relaxing, and sleeping.

Starfish House

Wet and wild

There are all kinds of things under the sea for **tourists** and divers to enjoy...

The underwater museum of art in Cancún, Mexico, showcases more than 500 sculptures on the seabed, and has an art gallery about protecting coral reefs.

The world's only underwater post office is located off Hideaway Island in the Pacific Ocean. Here, swimmers and snorkellers can send waterproof postcards.

It can be dangerous to come to the surface after a long time underwater. Pressure can build on the brain and nervous system.

Success story

In the 1960s, French explorer Jacques Cousteau designed underwater research stations. The first was a **small**, **steel cylinder**, with plenty of home comforts, including a television and radio.

Jacques Cousteau

Starfish House

The largest of Cousteau's research stations was Starfish House. It was shaped like a star and built on the bottom of the Red Sea. Jacques and his team used this as a base for a month to **study fish** and **ocean maps**. They had hot water, heaters, telephones, and record players.

In 2019, the world's biggest underwater restaurant opened in Norway. It has giant glass windows looking into the sea.

Now there is only one permanent underwater research base. Off the Florida Keys, USA, lies the Aquarius Reef Base, where scientists do research and astronauts prepare for space.

Work on the waves

Lots of people work beside, in, and on the ocean. For them, every day is an **adventure**!

Oil rig

Ocean conservationist

Humans harm the planet in many ways. A conservationist looks for ways to **protect** the environment.

Ocean engineer

An engineer **solves problems** and comes up with new ideas. An ocean engineer might help design and build an ocean rig for drilling oil.

Marine biologist

Studying the homes and behaviours of **animals** and **plants** is the job of a marine biologist.

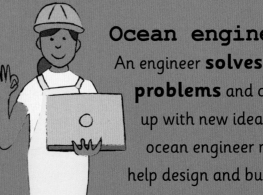

Microscope

Flask

Deep-sea diver

A diver is an **underwater explorer**. Divers can swim deep beneath the waves, filming fish, and exploring shipwrecks.

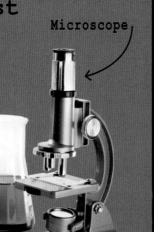

Ice see you!

People who work for the International Ice Patrol **tow** floating **icebergs** out of the way of oil rigs.

Coastguard helicopter

Aquatic vet

When a sea animal is **injured** or **sick**, an aquatic vet will come to the rescue!

Fisher

A fisher sails out to sea in a fishing boat to **catch** fish for your dinner.

Coastguard

The sea can be a dangerous place. A coastguard **rescues people** who need saving.

Oceanographer

An oceanographer uses scientific tools and technology to study the ocean and make **maps** of the ocean floor.

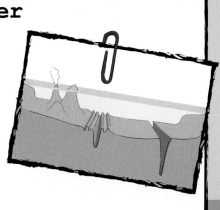

Marine mechanic

A marine mechanic checks and **repairs** all kinds of machines, including tiny boats and giant battleships.

Battleship

Ocean **rescue**

The ocean can be dangerous. Luckily, there are people doing things to try to make it **safer**.

Risky seas

When the first adventurers set out to sea, it was very **risky**. They faced deadly storms and rickety ships. Most adventurers couldn't swim, so they could drown. Today, trained lifeguards and coastguards rescue people who get into difficulty at sea.

In 1708, the first paid lifeguard station in the world was set up in China, on the banks of the Yangtze river.

The first lifeboat

You need an **unsinkable boat** to rescue a sinking ship or struggling swimmer. The first lifeboat was built after a disaster, where a ship hit the seabed and the crew drowned. The lifeboat was designed as part of a competition.

The first lifeboat.

TYNE

1st PRIZE

Today, boats have inflatable life rafts in case of an emergency.

THE REWARD

William Wouldhave and Henry Greathead took part in the first lifeboat competition. The reward was 2 guineas (around £2.10 or $2.91). The judges couldn't decide on a winner, so they took ideas from both men to create the final design. William Wouldhave was offended, so Henry Greathead was asked to build the lifeboat. Greathead is now known as the inventor of the lifeboat.

£2

10p

Adrift at sea

When a ship is floating and can't be steered or tied up, it is called adrift. Between 1813 and 1815, Japanese Captain Oguri Jukichi and Otokichi, one of his sailors, survived adrift at sea for a whopping **484 days** before they were rescued – that's the longest time adrift at sea!

They lived off soybeans and water.

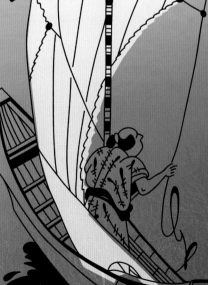

Sea supplies

The world's waters are busy places! From medicine and mining to transport and trade, the oceans have **supplies** and **services** that help people all over the world.

Marvellous medicines

Marine life can help make **medicines**. Cone snails have helped create painkillers, while sponges and corals have inspired new treatments for diseases.

Super-seaweed

The largest supplies of **seaweed** are grown in Asia. Farmers collect it to sell for food because it is very popular. Seaweed is also used as fuel, in plant fertiliser, and in skincare products.

Sea sponge

Cone snail

Seaweed

Wind turbines stand in the ocean, where their giant blades spin in strong winds. They make power, which is turned into electricity. Their energy is renewable, which means it will not run out.

Finding fuels

Oil and **natural gas** lie deep under the seabed inside layers of rock. These fuels can be reached by drilling. They provide sources of energy, but these fossil fuels will run out.

About 200 million containers a year are transported by cargo ships.

Salty seas

The ocean produces different **minerals**, including salt. For many years, people living on the coast have been using these salty waters to make edible salt.

Enormous cargo ships carry heavy loads across the ocean, in steel boxes that stack up like building bricks.

Fish, shellfish, and crustaceans are also huge food sources.

When seawater is evaporated, we can collect salt.

Fishy business

Who doesn't love a fish supper? But what are the dangers of fishing, and how can we **protect** our fishy friends for years to come?

Fishing industry

Millions of people make a living from fishing. This global industry produces **tonnes** of seafood each year.

Seafood diet

Seafood is an important source of **protein** that keeps our bodies strong and healthy. Oily fish, such as salmon, are good for boosting brain power.

Tempura prawns are rich in protein.

We can help by eating fish caught by people who ar

Trawler trouble

Big fishing boats called **trawlers** drag huge nets over the seabed and scoop up fish, but they can destroy the seabed and harm the animals that live there.

Trawler boat

Whales, dolphins, and turtles can get tangled up in fishing nets.

!

OVERFISHING
More than 400 marine species are endangered due to overfishing.

They are at it again!

Fish for the future

Overfishing is when too many fish are caught too quickly, leaving fish in danger of dying out. **Sustainable** fishing protects fish. They are caught at a slower rate, giving them time to breed and increase in number.

...working to PROTECT ocean habitats and marine life.

Ocean hazards

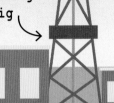
Offshore drilling rig

Our ocean is affected by **human activity**. As people disturb marine environments, the water and the wildlife suffer.

Hello? Can anyone hear me?

Endangered animals

People's actions are endangering the lives of marine creatures. **Noise** pollution has affected communication between grey whales, and **habitat loss** has left sea turtles without nesting sites.

Grey whale

For years, whales have been hunted for their meat, oil, and bones. There are now laws in place to stop whaling.

Drilling

Oil and natural gas are extracted from deep under the seabed. Drilling **disturbs** the surrounding environment and the creatures living there.

Brrrrrrrr

210

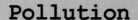
Oil tanker

Oil spills

If an oil tanker leaks, the spillage spreads throughout the water, polluting the ocean and **harming wildlife**.

Pollution

Many harmful things can pollute the ocean, such as rubbish and chemical fertilisers used by farmers. Toxic sewage systems can also **leak** into the water.

Oil coats the feathers of seabirds, making it difficult for them to stay afloat. They can also swallow the harmful oil when trying to get clean.

Trawler fishing boat

Trawler nets damage homes on the seabed.

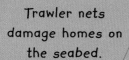

Making changes

Now for the good news! **New laws**, as well as conservation projects and campaigns, are helping to protect and preserve the ocean.

Climate change

Our planet is **warming up** more quickly than ever before. Humans are having a big impact, and the devastating effects can be seen in the ocean today.

Climate change causes EXTREME

Global warming

As natural resources are used up, harmful gases are released into the atmosphere. These gases trap heat and make the world hotter. This is called global warming and it causes disasters, such as **forest fires**.

Forest fire

Melting ice

Rising global temperatures are causing snow and ice to melt, and less ice to form in winter. Many polar animals are losing the ice they need to travel and hunt.

Polar bear

Carbon dioxide is absorbed by the ocean, making it more acidic. Many types of shellfish are dying as a result.

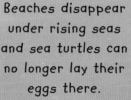

Where can we lay our eggs?

Beaches disappear under rising seas and sea turtles can no longer lay their eggs there.

weather, such as DROUGHTS and STORMS.

Rising sea levels

La Digue Island, Seychelles

As ice and snow continue to melt, the extra water makes sea levels rise. This puts some islands and coastlines, and the people living there, at risk of **flooding**.

Coral bleaching

As the ocean gets hotter, coral becomes stressed, **turns white**, and **dies**. This is called "coral bleaching", and it leaves many sea creatures homeless.

What's happened to my home?

Bleached coral

Plastic problems

Every year, **millions of tonnes** of plastic ends up in our oceans. It pollutes the water and is a danger to animals. But there's lots we can do to help!

Rubbish collection

The Great Pacific Garbage Patch is an enormous area of **plastic waste**, floating in the north Pacific Ocean. Currents move in a circle, causing rubbish to clump together and swirl around.

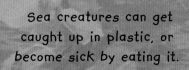

Sea creatures can get caught up in plastic, or become sick by eating it.

In pieces

Plastic breaks down into **microplastics**, bits of plastic that are about the size of a sesame seed. They are so tiny that sea creatures can swallow them, causing plastic to enter the food chain.

How to help

Plastic in the ocean is scary problem, but we can all help to **make it better**.

What is this strange new island in the Pacific Ocean?

Most plastic waste gets washed up onto beaches. Then beaches need to cleaned up by hand.

That's not a jellyfish!

Reduce
Avoid single-use plastics.

Recycle
Put waste in the recycling bin.

Re-use
Buy items that can be used again.

Clean up
Join a beach clean.

Saving our seas

A lot of people are working hard to **protect** our planet. From global charities to local communities, their work inspires us to do our bit to help.

Clean Seas campaign

In 2017, the United Nations (UN) launched the Clean Seas campaign, which brings people together to **reduce** the **plastic pollution** in the seas. Fifty-seven countries have joined the campaign!

SOS
Save our seas

There's no Planet-B

The Clean Seas campaign encourages recycling, and discourages the use of single-use plastics.

Marine reserves

Marine Protected Areas (MPAs) are areas in the ocean where **fishing** and **building** is **banned**, so that underwater habitats can thrive.

The Galápagos Marine Reserve surrounds the Galápagos Islands, in the Pacific Ocean. It is one of the largest and most diverse MPAs, with nearly 3,000 marine species.

More than 100 countries take part in the International Coastal Cleanup. People remove litter from beaches around the world.

Thank you!

PROTECTED AREA!

Amazing activists

Meet the people who are determined to **repair and revive** our oceans.

Sir David Attenborough

This natural historian loves our planet. His television series, *Blue Planet*, highlighted the problems our oceans face.

Greta Thunberg

Swedish teenager Greta is famous for her efforts to stop climate change. She demands leaders take action.

Kristal Ambrose

Caribbean activist Kristal set up the Bahamas Plastic Movement to find ways to reduce plastic pollution in the ocean.

Journey into the **unknown**

Most of Earth's oceans haven't been **explored** – yet! There's much more to discover, but we must also protect our wonderful waters for future generations to enjoy.

Deep-sea submersible

Oceana objective

Oceana is the biggest international organisation focusing on protecting the world's waters. Their goal is to protect **30 per cent** of the oceans by 2030.

Some organisations work to stop harmful activities, such as bottom trawling in protected areas.

Thinking about the future

Humans are causing problems for marine life. Supporting environmental projects and finding sustainable ways of living are essential for the future.

Life itself

Space exploration looks for life on other planets, but here on Earth, we still don't know exactly how and where life began! The oceans hold clues, so scientists are **diving down** for the answers.

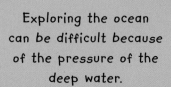

Exploring the ocean can be difficult because of the pressure of the deep water.

 Yeti crab

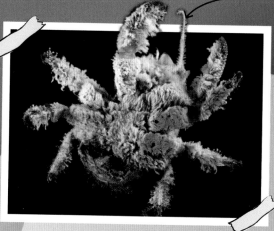

In 2005, the yeti crab was discovered in the Pacific Ocean.

Undiscovered species

The ocean is so big that it is hard to know **how many** marine creatures live there. Scientists think that 91 per cent of ocean species have yet to be named or discovered.

New MARINE LIFE is discovered EVERY DAY!

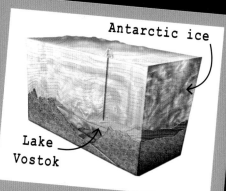

Antarctic ice

Lake Vostok

Water is still being discovered. In 1996, Lake Vostok was found beneath layers of Antarctic ice.

Index

Acknowledgements

The publisher would like to thank the following for their kind permission to reproduce their photographs:

(Key: a-above; b-below/bottom; c-centre; f-far; l-left; r-right; t-top)

1 123RF.com: lattesmile (br/fishes); Wilfred Marissen (tc). **Alamy Stock Photo:** blickwinkel / Mildenberger (cla). **Dreamstime.com:** Luna Vandoorne Vallejo / Lunavandoorne (bl); Tetiana Saranchuk (c/Seagull); Ylivdesign (br). **Shutterstock.com:** Eva Speshneva (c). **2 123RF.com:** lattesmile (br). **Alamy Stock Photo:** Brent Stephenson / Nature Picture Library (cra). **Getty Images / iStock:** GeorgePeters (crb). **naturepl.com:** Doug Perrine (tc). **3 123RF.com:** hatza (tc). **naturepl.com:** Gary Bell / Oceanwide (b). **4 Dreamstime.com:** Viacheslav Dubrovin (bl). **4-5 Alamy Stock Photo:** Norbert Probst / imageBROKER (bc). **5 123RF.com:** annaguz (bc). **Alamy Stock Photo:** Tony Wu / Nature Picture Library (tc). **6 Alamy Stock Photo:** Blue Planet Archive JCO (clb). **Dreamstime.com:** Kharlamova (bc). **6-7 123RF.com:** Prapan Ngawkeaw (b). **7 123RF.com:** vilainecrevette (cr). **Alamy Stock Photo:** Nature Picture Library (bl). **Dreamstime.com:** Kharlamova (cb). **naturepl.com:** Sue Daly (bc). **8 Alamy Stock Photo:** Brent Stephenson / Nature Picture Library (tl). **Dreamstime.com:** Kharlamova (c, br); Alexey Martynov (ca); Ponomarevaekaterina2015 (cb). **9 Shutterstock.com:** zabavina (ca). **10 Dreamstime.com:** Ponomarevaekaterina2015 (bc); Cat Vec (bl). **10-11 123RF.com:** 1xpert. **12 123RF.com:** Liliia Khuzhakhmetova / lilkin (ca, cra, bc); macrovector (cr). **Dreamstime.com:** Ernest Akayeu (c/surfing); Luciano Mortula (c); Olga Samorodova (c/Cartoon). **13 123RF.com:** Liliia Khuzhakhmetova / lilkin (c/cargo, cr, clb/cargo, cb/cargo); macrovector (cl/cartoon). **Dreamstime.com:** Ernest Akayeu (clb); Jemastock (cla); Rimma Z (ca); Dzianis Martynenka (cl); Antoniosantosg (c); Godruma (cb). **14 123RF.com:** Alhovik (c). **Dreamstime.com:** Sabelskaya (bc); Michael Zysman (tc/Iguana). **naturepl.com:** Solvin Zankl (cr). **Shutterstock.com:** 6x6x6 (tc); zabavina (bl). **15 Alamy Stock Photo:** Brent Stephenson / Nature Picture Library (cr). **Dreamstime.com:** Christopher Wood / Chriswood44 (tl); Mutabor5 (cla). **Shutterstock.com:** 6x6x6 (bc); Voropaev Vasiliy (c). **16 Dreamstime.com:** Borlili (clb). **18 Dreamstime.com:** Kenm (bl); Melonstone (cb). **18-19 123RF.com:** (t). **19 123RF.com:** bakai (clb); Mark Bowden (cb); mihtiander (cr). **Dreamstime.com:** Janos Gaspar (clb/Girl). **20 Dreamstime.com:** Daniel Eskridge (br); William Roberts (bl). **21 Dreamstime.com:** Mark Turner (bc). **22 123RF.com:** annaguz (ca). **Dreamstime.com:** John Anderson (cb); Kharlamova (cr); Microvone (clb, bc). **23 123RF.com:** annaguz (ca). **Alamy Stock Photo:** FB-Fischer / imageBROKER (tl); Jaime Franch Travel Photo (cr). **Dreamstime.com:** Artur Balytskyi (bl); Jacklooser (cb); Kharlamova (tc); Ylivdesign (br). **Science Photo Library:** Georgette Douwma (tc/Deep sea vents). **Shutterstock.com:** Eduard Radu (c). **24 123RF.com:** Robert McIntyre (cr). **Shutterstock.com:** Yongyut Kumsri (cl). **24-25 123RF.com:** lattesmile (b); Prapan Ngawkeaw (b/Sand). **25 123RF.com:** epicstockmedia (cr). **Alamy Stock Photo:** David Fleetham (tr); Richard Cummins / robertharding (clb). **Shutterstock.com:** Eva Speshneva (ca). **26 Alamy Stock Photo:** Ann Cutting (cb); Michael David Murphy (cb/port). **Shutterstock.com:** pimpisan02 (crb). **26-27 123RF.com:** Prapan Ngawkeaw (cb). **27 Alamy Stock Photo:** Grant Taylor (tl). **Dreamstime.com:** Yuliya Rudenko (br). **28-29 123RF.com:** Evgeni Bobrov (b). **29 123RF.com:** Liliia Khuzhakhmetova / lilkin (ca). **Alamy Stock Photo:** UrbanLife / Stockimo (tr). **30-31 123RF.com:** annaguz (b). **Dreamstime.com:** Astrofireball; Cornelius20 (ca); Vaclav Volrab (c); Microvone (b/Seaweeds); Alison Gibson (b/Line). **31 123RF.com:** annaguz (ca). **32 Alamy Stock Photo:** John Richmond (bc). **Dreamstime.com:** 64samcorp (tl, tr); Anna Cinaroglu (br). **33 123RF.com:** Ruslan Nassyrov (bc). **Alamy Stock Photo:** James Osmond Photography (bl); Michael Pitts / Nature Picture Library (tr). **Dreamstime.com:** Alisali (cla/chalk); Lehuishi (cla); Carafoto (tc); Nataliia Velishchuk (cra). **34 123RF.com:** Alhovik (tr). **Dreamstime.com:** Lavizzara (cl). **34-35 123RF.com:** Eero Oskari Porkka (c). **35 Alamy Stock Photo:** Olaf Krüger / imageBROKER (cla). **Dreamstime.com:** Andrey Armyagov (bl); Paul Topp / Nalukai (cr). **36-37 naturepl.com:** Doug Perrine (ca). **Shutterstock.com:** zabavina (t). **36 123RF.com:** lattesmile (c). **Dreamstime.com:** John Anderson (cb); Dongfan Wang / Tabgac (cr). **naturepl.com:** Gary Bell / Oceanwide (bc). **37 Alamy Stock Photo:** Reinhard Dirscherl (bl). **Dreamstime.com:** Kotomiti_okuma (c). **38 123RF.com:** Richard Whitcombe / whitcomberd (b). **Alamy Stock Photo:** Science History Images (cra). **Dorling Kindersley:** Natural History Museum, London (clb). **39 Alamy Stock Photo:** Solvin Zankl / mauritius images GmbH (cla); Andrey Nekrasov / imageBROKER; Paul R. Sterry / Nature Photographers Ltd (br). **40 Alamy Stock Photo:** Norbert Probst / imageBROKER (cr). **Dreamstime.com:** John Anderson (cl). **40-41 123RF.com:** Vadym Kurgak. **Dreamstime.com:** Pavel Naumov (tc); Seadam (b). **41 Alamy Stock Photo:** lcrms (tc). **naturepl.com:** David Shale (tr). **42 Science Photo Library:** Kelvin Aitken, VW Pics (r). **43 Alamy Stock Photo:** Everett Collection Historical (br); Tony Wu / Nature Picture Library (cb). **Dreamstime.com:** Showvector (bl). **naturepl.com:** Brandon Cole (clb); Nick Hawkins (tl); Alex Mustard (tr); Magnus Lundgren (crb). **Science Photo Library:** M.P. O'Neill (cb/Cannonball Jellyfish). **44 Dreamstime.com:** Elisei Shafer (clb). **45 Alamy Stock Photo:** blickwinkel / F. Hecker (cla); Sue Daly / Nature Picture Library (tc). **46 Dreamstime.com:** Shane Myers (br). **47 123RF.com:** Iuliia Grebeniukova / SolntseRA (cb). **Dreamstime.com:** Jianghongyan (clb). **48 Dreamstime.com:** Liliia Khuzhakhmetova / lilkin (cra). **48-49 Alamy Stock Photo:** WaterFrame (c). **49 123RF.com:** natchapohn (bc). **Alamy Stock Photo:** Xinhua (c). **Dorling Kindersley:** Natural History Museum, London (br). **50 Dreamstime.com:** Jianghongyan (cla); Valentyn75 (crb). **50-51 Dreamstime.com:** Allexxandar. **51 123RF.com:** Hans Geel (ca). **Dorling Kindersley:** Natural History Museum, London (cla). **Dreamstime.com:** Ethan Daniels (br); Yodsawaj Suriyasirisin (bl). **52 123RF.com:** annaguz (tr). **Dreamstime.com:** Skypixel (crb). **naturepl.com:** Doug Perrine (cl); David Shale (br). **52-53 Dreamstime.com:** Blueringmedia. **53 Alamy Stock Photo:** Mark Conlin (tl). **Shutterstock.com:** Sunnydream (cb). **54-55 Dreamstime.com:** Seadam (t). **naturepl.com:** Sue Daly. **55 Alamy Stock Photo:** Jeff Rotman / Nature Picture Library (tl). **Dreamstime.com:** Aleaders (cr). **naturepl.com:** Brandon Cole (bl). **56 Alamy Stock Photo:** David Massemin / Biosphoto (crb); blickwinkel / Mildenberger (cb). **Science Photo Library:** Alexander Semenov (cr). **56-57 Dreamstime.com:** Seadam. **57 naturepl.com:** Pascal Kobeh (cra); Doug Perrine (clb). **Shutterstock.com:** unterwegs (crb). **58 Alamy Stock Photo:** Anup Shah / Nature Picture Library (bl). **Dorling Kindersley:** Natural History Museum, London (cla). **Dreamstime.com:** Cmeili87 (cr). **Getty Images / iStock:** danilovi (crb). **59 Alamy Stock Photo:** Reinhard Dirscherl (cl, br); Doug Perrine (bl). **Dreamstime.com:** Donyanedomam (cra). **60 Dreamstime.com:** Fireflamenco (bl, br). **60-61 naturepl.com:** Pete Oxford. **61 123RF.com:** lattesmile (c, clb). **Dreamstime.com:** Viacheslav Dubrovin (cr); Fireflamenco (bl). **Getty Images:** M.M. Sweet (tl). **naturepl.com:** Doug Perrine (ca). **62 Dorling Kindersley:** Natural History Museum (bl). **62-63 Dreamstime.com:** Lunamarina. **64 Dreamstime.com:** Alexey Martynov (tr). **Shutterstock.com:** Good luck images (cra); Kaschibo (bl); MyImages - Micha (br). **64-65 Dreamstime.com:** Andreykuzmin. **65 Dreamstime.com:** Alexey Martynov (tc); Dongfan Wang / Tabgac (cla); Iryna Verhelesova (cb). **naturepl.com:** Ralph Pace (bl). **Shutterstock.com:** Gena Melendrez (cr); Vovantarakan (cb/lamprey river). **67 Alamy Stock Photo:** Alex Mustard / Nature Picture Library (cla). **naturepl.com:** Franco Banfi (cra); Tony Wu (crb). **68-69 Dreamstime.com:** Andreykuzmin. **68 naturepl.com:** Norbert Wu (br). **69 naturepl.com:** Gary Bell / Oceanwide (c). **70 Alamy Stock Photo:** Marty Snyderman / Stephen Frink Collection (br). **Dreamstime.com:** Vladvitek (clb). **71 Alamy Stock Photo:** Blue Planet Archive JMI (clb). **Dorling Kindersley:** Natural History Museum (cr). **72-73 123RF.com:** Olga Khoroshunova (t). **72 Alamy Stock Photo:** Blickwinkel / F. Hecker (bc); Reinhard Dirscherl (cra); Wildlife Gmbh (c). **73 Alamy Stock Photo:** Josef Beck / imageBROKER (ca); Michael Wood / Stocktrek Images (bl). **FLPA:** Norbert Wu / Minden Pictures (crb). **74 Dreamstime.com:** Kharlamova (bl). **74-75 Alamy Stock Photo:** Martin Strmiska. **75 123RF.com:** Willyambradberry (br). **Dreamstime.com:** Blue Ring Education Pte Ltd (cra). **Science Photo Library:** Christopher Swann (tl). **Shutterstock.com:** Eva Speshneva (ca). **76 123RF.com:** Witold Kaszkin (tl). **Alamy Stock Photo:** WaterFrame_fba (cb). **Dreamstime.com:** Luna Vandoorne Vallejo / Lunavandoorne (clb); Nataliia Velishchuk (crb). **77 Alamy Stock Photo:** Andrey Nekrasov / imageBROKER (cb). **naturepl.com:** Martin Camm / Carwardine (bc); Doug Perrine (tc). **78 Alamy Stock Photo:** Jean-Paul Ferrero / AUSCAPE / Auscape International Pty Ltd (clb). **78-79 Alamy Stock Photo:** Franco Banfi / Nature Picture Library (c). **79 Alamy Stock Photo:** Mark Carwardine / Nature Picture Library (tl). **80-81 Alamy Stock Photo:** Dotted Zebra. **81 123RF.com:** alfadanz (crb, b); natchapohn (cr). **Dreamstime.com:** Planetfelicity (cla). **82 Dreamstime.com:** Vladimir Melnik / Zanskar (cra). **Fotolia:** Vladimir Melnik (br). **83 Alamy Stock Photo:** Sylvain Cordier / Biosphoto (cr). **Getty Images / iStock:** pum_eva (cra); slowmotiongli (b); Michael Zeigler (ca). **84-85 Dorling Kindersley:** Frank Greenaway (c, bc). **Dreamstime.com:** Leonello Calvetti / Leocalvett. **85 Dreamstime.com:** Rizikpic (bl); Willtu (ca). **Getty Images:** Fuse (cra). **86 Alamy Stock Photo:** Andy Trowbridge / Nature Picture Library (bc). **Dreamstime.com:** Donyanedomam (cl). **Shutterstock.com:** zabavina (cra). **87 123RF.com:** Wilfred Marissen (br). **Alamy Stock Photo:** Tui De Roy / Nature Picture Library (t); Brent Stephenson / Nature Picture Library (cb). **Shutterstock.com:** zabavina (bl). **88 123RF.com:** natchapohn (clb). **Dreamstime.com:** Alexander Shalamov / Alexshalamov (cl); Vectorikart (bl); Denis Dubrovin / Denisdubrovin (tr); Izanbar (cr). **88-89 Dreamstime.com:** Allexxandar. **89 Getty Images / iStock:** Grafner (b). **naturepl.com:** Flip Nicklin (cra). **90-91 123RF.com:** Prapan Ngawkeaw (b). **90 123RF.com:** Roman kalnenko (bc). **Alamy Stock Photo:** Gregory Gard (c). **Dreamstime.com:** Andreistanescu (clb); Donyanedomam (tr); Frank Fichtmueller (cla); Rafal Stachura (cb); Callum Redgrave Close (bl). **91 Alamy Stock Photo:** Melba Photo Agency (cb/sea star); Nature Picture Library (clb). **Getty Images / iStock:** clintscholz (cr). **naturepl.com:** Flip Nicklin (cl); Kirkendall-Spring (cb); Jeff Rotman (crb). **Science Photo Library:** Simon Fraser (tl). **92 123RF.com:** lynxtime (tc). **Alamy Stock Photo:** James Osmond (bl). **93 Alamy Stock Photo:** Mark van Veen / Buiten-Beeld (cl); Clarence Holmes Wildlife (c); De Meester Johan / Arterra Picture Library (bl); Ernie Janes (bl/Marshes). **Dreamstime.com:** Supertrooper / alex (fbl); Javarman (br). **94 123RF.com:** Engdao Wichitpunya (b). **94-95 Dreamstime.com:** Seadam. **95 123RF.com:** feathercollector (ca). **Alamy Stock Photo:** Jurgen Freund / Nature Picture Library (tr). **Dreamstime.com:** Leung Cho Pan / Leungchopan (bl). **96 Dreamstime.com:** Vectorikart (br). **96-97 Alamy Stock Photo:** Stephen Frink / Stephen Frink Collection (ca). **Dreamstime.com:** Vladimir Surkov / Surkov_vladimir (t). **97 Alamy Stock Photo:** Blue Planet Archive JCO (t); Francis Abbott / Nature Picture Library (bc); Frank Hecker (br). **Dreamstime.com:** Seadam (cl). **98-99 naturepl.com:** Flip Nicklin. **99 Dreamstime.com:** Izanbar (c). **naturepl.com:** Suzi Eszterhas (br); Ralph Pace (tr). **100-101 Dreamstime.com:** Seadam (cb). **100 Alamy Stock Photo:** Howard Chew (bl). **Dreamstime.com:** Jemma Craig (clb). **101 Dreamstime.com:** Deborah Coles (br); Ten Theeralerttham / rawangtak (crb); Wirestock (clb). **Getty Images:** Daniel Osterkamp (cr). **102 123RF.com:** Olga Khoroshunova / goodolga (bc). **Dorling Kindersley:** Linda Pitkin (bc/flatworm, bc/Feather star). **Dreamstime.com:** Jeremy Brown (br); Mrhanson (cla). **Getty Images / iStock:** vlad61 (l). **103 Dorling Kindersley:** Jerry Young (cla, cb). **Dreamstime.com:** Alexander Shalamov / Alexshalamov (cra); Kevin Panizza / Kpanizza (cr); Petr Zamecnik (bc). **Getty Images / iStock:** Ultramarinfoto (br). **104-105 Getty Images / iStock:** RomoloTavani. **104 Alamy Stock Photo:** Norbert Probst / imageBROKER (bl). **Getty Images / iStock:** PongMoji (cr). **105 Alamy Stock Photo:** Marevision / agefotostock (bl); J.W.Alker / imageBROKER (ca). **Dreamstime.com:** Seadam (cr). **106 123RF.com:** lynxtime (cra). **Alamy Stock Photo:** Joseph C. Dovala / agefotostock (b); Paulo Oliveira (cr). **107 Alamy Stock Photo:** Helmut Corneli (b); Jeff Milisen (cr). **FLPA:** Imagebroker,Helmut Corneli / Imagebroker (bl). **108 naturepl.com:** Bryan and Cherry Alexander (br). **109 123RF.com:** Michal Balada (crb); Sergeyp (tl/Texture). **Alamy Stock Photo:** Diana Johanna Velasquez (bc). **Dreamstime.com:** Adeliepenguin (br); Checco (cr). **naturepl.com:** Norbert Wu (cl). **Shutterstock.com:** NiarKrad (cra); zabavina (tl). **110 123RF.com:** Eric Isselee / isselee (cr). **110-111 Dorling Kindersley:** Jerry Young (c). **111 Dreamstime.com:** Eric Isselée / Isselee (c). **Getty Images:** Purestock (crb). **Getty Images / iStock:** twphotos (cra). **112 123RF.com:** natchapohn (bl). **Alamy Stock Photo:** Oceans Image / Avalon.red (bl/Antarctic krill); Paulo Oliveira (crb). **Dreamstime.com:** Kotomiti_okuma (fcl); Jan Martin Will (cl); Tarpan (cr). **113 Alamy Stock Photo:** David Tipling / David Tipling Photo Library (cla); Marko Steffensen (clb). **Dreamstime.com:** Denis Dubrovin / Denisdubrovin (ca); Tarpan (cr). **114 123RF.com:** Pavlo Vakhrushev / vapi (ca). **Alamy Stock Photo:** David Shale / Nature Picture Library (cr, fcr). **Dreamstime.com:** Shane Myers (bl); Neirfy (cla); Cat Vec (cb).

naturepl.com: Florian Graner (crb); Solvin Zankl (cra). **Shutterstock.com:** MyImages - Micha (c). **114-115 Alamy Stock Photo:** Wolfgang Pölzer (bc). **115 Alamy Stock Photo:** Ethan Daniels (cb/sea pen); NOAA (ca); David Shale / Nature Picture Library (cb, c/Sea cucumber). **naturepl.com:** Gary Bell / Oceanwide (cla); Doc White (cla/Pelican); David Shale (ca/Viperfish); Norbert Wu (c). **Science Photo Library:** British Antarctic Survey (cr); Dante Fenolio (ca/Shrimp, cb/Tripod Fish); Wim Van Egmond (cra); David Shale / Nature Picture Library (cr/anthomedusa, fcr). **116 Dreamstime.com:** Wrangel (bl). **116-117 123RF.com:** Ihor Bondarenko (c/Green algae). **Dreamstime.com:** Sabri Deniz Kizil / Bogalo; Martin Voeller (c). **117 123RF.com:** Micha Klootwijk / michaklootwijk (cr). **Alamy Stock Photo:** Mathieu Foulquie / Biosphoto (cla/Sargassum); Wildestanimal (cl); WaterFrame_dpr (br). **Dreamstime.com:** Vectorikart (cla). **118-119 Dreamstime.com:** Sabri Deniz Kizil / Bogalo. **118 Alamy Stock Photo:** BJ Warnick / Newscom (c); Paulo Oliveira (bl). **Dreamstime.com:** Vectorikart (crb). **119 Alamy Stock Photo:** David Fleetham (ca); Paulo Oliveira (cra); David Shale / Nature Picture Library (cla). **Dreamstime.com:** Igor Zubkov (tc, cr, b); Zweizug (cb). **120-121 Getty Images / iStock:** PawelG Photo (t). **120 Alamy Stock Photo:** Buena Vista Pictures / Courtesy Everett Collection. **121 Alamy Stock Photo:** Paulo Oliveira (ca, cb). **naturepl.com:** Norbert Wu (c). **122-123 Dreamstime.com:** Vultur Dana Mihaela (c). **122 Alamy Stock Photo:** David Shale / Nature Picture Library (bc); The Natural History Museum (clb). **Dreamstime.com:** Greg Amptman (cr). **123 Alamy Stock Photo:** Mathieu Foulquie / Biosphoto (tl); BJ Warnick / Newscom (ca); Ethan Daniels (cb). **Dreamstime.com:** Greg Amptman (bl); Selvam Raghupathy (r/background). **Science Photo Library:** British Antarctic Survey (r). **124 Getty Images:** Alastair Pollock Photography (tc). **Science Photo Library:** Christopher Swann (b). **125 123RF.com:** natchapohn (br). Alamy Stock Photo: Zoonar / Fritz Poelking (cra). **126 Alamy Stock Photo:** Brook Peterson / Stocktrek Images (cl); Zoonar / Fritz Poelking (cr). **127 Alamy Stock Photo:** Gerard Lacz / mauritius images GmbH (tl); Reinhard Dirscherl / mauritius images GmbH (tr). **Dreamstime.com:** Rinus Baak (br); Josephine Julian Lobijin (bl). **128 Dreamstime.com:** Simon Eeman (br); Ymgerman (bl). **129 Alamy Stock Photo:** Ahmed Areef (tr); Zoonar / Simon Eeman (clb). **Dreamstime.com:** Jakub Gojda (br). **naturepl.com:** Fabrice Cahez (tl); Pete Oxford (tl/beach); Phil Chapman (cra). **130 Alamy Stock Photo:** Brandon Cole Marine Photography (tr). **130-131 Dorling Kindersley:** Jerry Young (Neon tetras). **Getty Images:** Alastair Pollock Photography (c). **131 123RF.com:** Nicholas Toh (cr); vilainecrevette. **Alamy Stock Photo:** blickwinkel / H. Schmidbauer (ca). **Dreamstime.com:** Hotshotsworldwide (tc); Shane Myers (fbr). **Photolibrary:** Photodisc / White (br). **132-133 Dreamstime.com:** Zoom-zoom (t). **Science Photo Library:** Christopher Swann (b). **132 Alamy Stock Photo:** Jurgen Freund / Nature Picture Library (cl). **133 Science Photo Library:** Richard Brooks (c); Christopher Swann (cr). **134 Dreamstime.com:** Song Heming (bc). **135 123RF.com:** natchapohn (ca). **Dreamstime.com:** Iakov Filimonov (br); Mikhail Laptev (bl); Teguh Tirtaputra / Teguhtirta (cb); Piyathep (c). **Getty Images / iStock:** tiler84 (cla). **136 Dreamstime.com:** Fototrips (bl). **137 123RF.com:** Prapan Ngawkeaw (bl/Sand). **Dreamstime.com:** Jameschipper (tr); Mikhail Sokolov (crb). **Getty Images / iStock:** GeorgePeters (c). **Shutterstock.com:** George J (bl); Atomic Roderick (br). **138 Dreamstime.com:** Alevtina Tarasova (tc). **Shutterstock.com:** Davidhoffmann Photography (cl); Napat (bc). **139 Alamy Stock Photo:** Tony Wu / Nature Picture Library (cb). **Dreamstime.com:** Alevtina Tarasova (tl, cla, cra). **Shutterstock.com:** 6x6x6 (tr). **140 Alamy Stock Photo:** Blickwinkel / Hartl (cra); WaterFrame_fba (cr). **Getty Images / iStock:** Tonaquatic (clb, cb). **141 123RF.com:** Roy Longmuir / Brochman (cla). **Alamy Stock Photo:** Andrey Nekrasov (cl). **Dreamstime.com:** Linda Bucklin (bl); Sergey Uryadnikov / Surz01 (cra). **142 Dreamstime.com:** R. Gino Santa Maria / Shutterfree,LLC / Ginosphotos / Shutterfree,Llc (cl); Vectorikart (br). **142-143 Alamy Stock Photo:** NASA Photo (b); sheris (c). **143 Alamy Stock Photo:** Scenics & Science (ca). **144 123RF.com:** annaguz (bc). **Dreamstime.com:** Showvector (crb). **naturepl.com:** Gary Bell / Oceanwide (clb). **Shutterstock.com:** wildestanimal (cla). **144-145 Dreamstime.com:** Allexxandar. **145 Alamy Stock Photo:** Genevieve Vallee (clb). **Dreamstime.com:** Showvector (tl). **Science Photo Library:** Reinhard Dirscherl (t). **Shutterstock.com:** Gerald Robert Fischer (cb). **146 Alamy Stock Photo:** Matthew Banks (clb). **Dreamstime.com:** Kharlamova (bl). **naturepl.com:** Sue Daly (br). **Shutterstock.com:** Richard Whitcombe (cr). **147 Dreamstime.com:** Allnaturalbeth (c); Galinasavina (crb). **Shutterstock.com:** Alexandra HB (tc). **148 123RF.com:** kwiktor (crb). **naturepl.com:** Peter Scoones (cl). **Science Photo Library:** Georgette Douwma (clb); Andrew J. Martinez (cr). **149 123RF.com:** Richard Whitcombe (clb). **Alamy Stock Photo:** Nico van Kappel / Buiten-Beeld (crb). **Dreamstime.com:** Kjersti Joergensen. **150 123RF.com:** Rueangrit Srisuk (br). **Alamy Stock Photo:** WaterFrame_ase (r). **151 Alamy Stock Photo:** Paulo Oliveira (crb); Scenics & Science (cra); Solvin Zankl (clb). **Getty Images / iStock:** LPETTET (bc); PawelG Photo (t); RugliG (cla). **152 123RF.com:** Eric Isselee / isselee (bc/clownfish). **Dreamstime.com:** Michael Elliott (bl); Lightkitegirl (bc). **153 Alamy Stock Photo:** Norbert Probst / imageBROKER (crb); Don Mammoser (tl); Jennifer Idol / Stocktrek Images (bl). **Dreamstime.com:** Nikolai Sorokin (br). **154 Dreamstime.com:** Zweizug (tr). **154-155 123RF.com:** Prapan Ngawkeaw (b). **Dreamstime.com:** Pavel Naumov. **155 123RF.com:** hatza (fbl). **naturepl.com:** Sue Daly (bl). **156 Dreamstime.com:** Punnawich Limparungpatanakij (bl). **Shutterstock.com:** Inkley Studio (cla). **157 Dreamstime.com:** Gmm2000 (r). **Science Photo Library:** Thomas & Pat Leeson (bc). **158 123RF.com:** macrovector (c/cartoon). **Alamy Stock Photo:** Chronicle (crb). **Dreamstime.com:** Patrick Guenette (cb); Dave Jones / Lina Sipelyte (tl); Tomacco (cla). **Fotolia:** Dariusz Kopestynski (c). **Shutterstock.com:** Eva Speshneva (cl). **159 Dreamstime.com:** Ratz Attila (cla); Subbotina (bc/Sand). **Shutterstock.com:** Marish (bc). **160 Alamy Stock Photo:** INTERFOTO (cb). **Dorling Kindersley:** University of Pennsylvania Museum of Archaeology and Anthropology (bl). **161 Alamy Stock Photo:** Roy Langstaff (bc). **Dorling Kindersley:** Pitt Rivers Museum, University of Oxford (br). **Dreamstime.com:** Ivansmuk (cra). **162-163 Dreamstime.com:** Vyychan (Background). **162 Alamy Stock Photo:** Doug Houghton (fcl); van der Meer Marica / Arterra Picture Library (br). **Dreamstime.com:** Bjorn Hovdal (clb); Rodho (tr, cb); Joingate (cra); Igor Nikolayev (c); Volodymyr Pishchanyi (fcl/silver bars); Andrew Unangst (cl). **163 123RF.com:** macrovector (clb/cartoon). **Alamy Stock Photo:** Granger Historical Picture Archive (cr). **Dreamstime.com:** Chokchai Namthip (clb); Igor Nikolayev (ca, cl); Rodho (cb); Serezniy (br). **Fotolia:** Dariusz Kopestynski (cb/ship). **164 Alamy Stock Photo:** Ancient Art and Architecture (br); Alexandre Fagundes (cl); Artokoloro (bc). **Dreamstime.com:** Arsty (tl); Janusz Pieńkowski (c). **Shutterstock.com:** Studio_G (cr). **165 Alamy Stock Photo:** Chronicle (clb); Lebrecht Music & Arts (tr); Colport (cr); Interfoto / Personalities (crb). **Dreamstime.com:** Naci Yavuz (cla). **166 Alamy Stock Photo:** Prisma Archivo (br). **Dreamstime.com:** Isselee (fcl); Subbotina (cl/Sand). **Getty Images / iStock:** mccluremr (cl). **166-167 Dreamstime.com:** Subbotina (ca). **167 Alamy Stock Photo:** The Natural History Museum (tr). **Dreamstime.com:** Subbotina (br). **Getty Images / iStock:** Grafissimo (c). **168 Alamy Stock Photo:** Chronicle (cr). **Dreamstime.com:** Patrick Guenette (cb). **169 Alamy Stock Photo:** Chronicle (tl); Rob Powell (cr). **Shutterstock.com:** Eva Speshneva (ca). **170-171 123RF.com:** Sergey Oganesov / ensiferum (t). **Getty Images / iStock:** Extreme-Photographer (c). **170 123RF.com:** Anton Lunkov / antonlunkov (bl). **171 Alamy Stock Photo:** Imaginechina Limited (bl); Pictures Now (cr). **172 123RF.com:** Eric Isselee (bl). **Dreamstime.com:** Tomacco (cl). **Shutterstock.com:** Marish (crb). **173 Alamy Stock Photo:** IanDagnall Computing (bl). **Dreamstime.com:** Andreykuzmin (b); Ratz Attila (tc). **Shutterstock.com:** Marish (cb). **174 Alamy Stock Photo:** Historic Collection (cb); Louise Murray (cr). **175 Alamy Stock Photo:** AF Fotografie (cra); Lebrecht Music & Arts (cb). **Bridgeman Images:** (cla). **177 Alamy Stock Photo:** ITAR-TASS News Agency (cr); PJF Military Collection (cb); ZUMA Press, Inc. (br). **Dreamstime.com:** Attila Jandi (tl). **178 123RF.com:** Pawe? Szczepa?ski / pablo1960 (c). **Alamy Stock Photo:** ICP / incamerastock (b). **179 123RF.com:** Kittipong Jirasukhanont (tc). **Dreamstime.com:** Andrea Crisante / Homeworks255 (cr). **FLPA:** Flip Nicklin (cl). **Getty Images / iStock:** JackF (br). **180 123RF.com:** annaguz (clb, cb). **Dorling Kindersley:** Natural History Museum, London (cr). **Science Photo Library:** Natural History Museum, London (c, crb). **180-181 Dreamstime.com:** Alison Gibson. **181 123RF.com:** annaguz (bl). **Alamy Stock Photo:** Granger Historical Picture Archive (clb); Fraser Gray (cra). **Dreamstime.com:** Jose Tejo / Joetex1 (bc). **Science Photo Library:** (tc). **182 Alamy Stock Photo:** Artokoloro (cra); incamerastock (tc); World History Archive (cb); Jane Gould (bc). **Dreamstime.com:** Alexstar (tr). **183 Alamy Stock Photo:** Artmedia (cb); Actep Burstov (tl); Chronicle (cr, br, tr). **Dorling Kindersley:** NASA: Earth Observatory / NOAA (ca). **184-185 Getty Images / iStock:** ratpack223 (t, b). **184 Dreamstime.com:** Selvam Raghupathy (t); Anatoli Styf (c). **185 Alamy Stock Photo:** BNA Photographic (tc); Horia Bogdan (tr); Paul R. Sterry / Nature Photographers Ltd (cra). **186 NOAA:** (tr). **187 Alamy Stock Photo:** World History Archive (br). **188 Alamy Stock Photo:** Stuart F. Westmorland / Danita Delimont. **189 123RF.com:** pinipin (crb). **Dorling Kindersley:** Linda Pitkin (cr). **Dreamstime.com:** BY (bc); Jolanta Wojcicka (cra). **Getty Images / iStock:** ratpack223 (fcr). **190 Alamy Stock Photo:** Everett Collection Inc (cb); NASA Photo (c). **Dreamstime.com:** Andreykuzmin (cl, br); Tetiana Kozachok (tl); Fotofjodor (crb). **Getty Images / iStock:** marrio31 (fbl). **191 Alamy Stock Photo:** Pictorial Press Ltd (tc); Universal Art Archive (cl). **Dreamstime.com:** Andreykuzmin (tr, c); Fotofjodor (bc). **Getty Images / iStock:** CoreyFord (cb). **192 Alamy Stock Photo:** Gareth Fuller / PA Images (bc). **193 Alamy Stock Photo:** Sergio Moraes / Reuters (bc); Adrian Sherratt (c); UPI Photo / Terry Schmitt (br). **Dreamstime.com:** Juri Samsonov (cr). **Getty Images:** Shaun Botterill (bl). **194-195 Dreamstime.com:** Cornelius20; Alison Gibson (b). **194 123RF.com:** lattesmile (clb); Liliia Khuzhakhmetova / lilkin (ca). **Alamy Stock Photo:** Paulo Oliveira (br **Dreamstime.com:** Tetiana Saranchuk (crb); Trondur (tl). **195 123RF.com:** lattesmile (bl); Oleg Zhukov (tl). **Alamy Stock Photo:** Dino Fracchia (cr); Paulo Oliveira (br). **Dreamstime.com:** Denis Dubrovin / Denisdubrovin (c); Ken Backer / Sunguy (ca). **Getty Images / iStock:** photo5963 (tc). **196 123RF.com:** Oleg Zhukov (c). **197 Dreamstime.com:** Seadam (r). **198 123RF.com:** Gerold Grotelueschen (bc). **Dreamstime.com:** Kharlamova (br); Evgenii Naumov (cl, tr); Tomas Marek (cr). **198-199 123RF.com:** teodora1. **199 123RF.com:** martm (br); Sergei Uriadnikov (clb). **Alamy Stock Photo:** Nikki Bingham (cr PREVOST Vincent / hemis.fr (tl). **Dreamstime.com:** Kharlamova (ca); Sean Pavone (cra); Evgenii Naumov (bc). **200-201 Dreamstime.com:** Photoeuphoria (t). **200 Alamy Stock Photo:** Claudio Contreras / Nature Picture Library (bl); Paul Abbitt Rml (br). **201 Alamy Stock Photo:** DPA Picture Alliance (clb); Dino Fracchia (tr); Stephen Frink Collection (br). **202 Dreamstime.com:** Dmitriy Melnikov / Dgm007 (bc); Trondur (cra). **203 123RF.com:** Liliia Khuzhakhmetova / lilkin (ca Natalia Romanova (cla). **Dorling Kindersley:** Vikings of Middle England (c). **Dreamstime.com:** Ken Backer / Sunguy (cra). **204 Dreamstime.com:** Denis Dubrovin / Denisdubrovin (ca, clb, bc); Chur Guo (bl); David Morton (crb); Excentro (crb/Ribbon). **204-205 Dreamstime.com:** Cornelius20; Denis Dubrovin / Denisdubrovin (bc) **205 123RF.com:** salamatik (bc). **Dreamstime.com:** Denis Dubrovin Denisdubrovin (ca); Pe3ak (br). **206 123RF.com:** Liliia Khuzhakhmeto / lilkin (cra). **Dorling Kindersley:** Natural History Museum, London (bc). **207 123RF.com:** Liliia Khuzhakhmetova / lilkin (c). **Dreamstime.com:** Vectorikart (bc). **Getty Images / iStock:** photo5963 (cl). **208-209 Dreamstime.com:** Alison Gibson (c). **208 Dreamstime.com:** Christopher Elwell (bl). **209 123RF.com:** Liliia Khuzhakhmetov lilkin (ca). **210 Alamy Stock Photo:** Chronicle (cb). **Dorling Kindersley:** Natural History Museum, London (cl); Jerry Young (crb). **210-211 Dreamstime.com:** Cristina Bernhardsen (b). **211 Dorling Kindersley:** Linda Pitkin (clb/parrotfish); Jerry Young (cb). **Dreamstime.com:** Hadot (clb). **Getty Images / iStock:** cmturkme (tr); Nerthuz (tc). **212 Alamy Stock Photo:** Wayne Lynch / All Cana Photos (br). **Dreamstime.com:** Elantsev (bl). **212-213 123RF.com:** (sky); Sergey Nivens / nexusplexus (t). **213 123RF.com:** Anna Zakharchenko (cra). **Alamy Stock Photo:** Pascal Kobeh / Nature Picture Library (tl). **Dreamstime.com:** Hadot (cra/turtle); Melvinlee (**Getty Images / iStock:** NatureNow (clb). **214-215 Alamy Stock Photo:** Paulo Oliveira (ca). **naturepl.com:** Gary Bell / Oceanwide (c). **214 123RF.com:** lattesmile (crb). **Alamy Stock Photo:** Paulo Olive (bl). **215 Alamy Stock Photo:** Iain Masterton (tr). **Dreamstime.com:** Viacheslav Dubrovin (c); Tetiana Saranchuk (tc). **216 Dreamstime.com:** Viacheslav Dubrovin (cr/Sea turtle); Kharlamova (br). **naturepl.com:** Shane Gross (cra); Pete Oxford (cr). **216-217 123RF.com:** Volodymyr Golubyev (bc); meseberg; lattesmile (c). **217 Alamy Stock Photo:** IPA / Independent Photo Agency Srl (c); Tabat Fireman / Female Perspective (cra). **Elyse Butler:** (br). **Shutterstock.com:** wildestanimal (cla). **218 Alamy Stock Photo:** Jeff Rotman / Nature Picture Library (cr). **Getty Images / iStock:** doodlemachine. **219 Alamy Stock Photo:** Jeff Rotman / Nature Picture Library (bl, Science History Images (crb). **naturepl.com:** David Shale (cl). **220 123RF.com:** lattesmile (br). **Dreamstime.com:** Fotofjodor (bc); Izanbar (bl). **221 Alamy Stock Photo:** Melba Photo Agency (cra). **Dreamstime.com:** Fotofjodor (bl). **naturepl.com:** Doug Perrine (b) **222 Dreamstime.com:** Kharlamova (br); Shane Myers (bl). **223 123RF.com:** lattesmile (bc). **Alamy Stock Photo:** Lebrecht Music & Arts (bl). **Dreamstime.com:** Dongfan Wang / Tabgac (cl). **224 123RF.com:** lattesmile (b). **Dreamstime.com:** Dongfan Wang / Tabgac (bl). **Shutterstock.com:** Good luck images (crb)

Cover images: Front: **Dreamstime.com:** Eric Isselee bc, Dongfan Wang / Tabgac cr; **Getty Images / iStock:** GeorgePeters cla, vlad6 Back: **123RF.com:** Mike Price / mhprice tr; **Dorling Kindersley:** Lin Pitkin bl, Jerry Young cla; **Dreamstime.com:** Digitalbalance cla/(jellyfish), Fenkie Sumolang / Fenkieandreas crb

All other images © Dorling Kindersley
For further information see: www.dkimages.com

DK would like to thank:
Polly Goodman for proofreading; Marie Lorimer for the index; Polly Appleton for additional design; Sophie Parkes and Robin Moul for additional editing; Mrinmoy Mazumdar for DTP design; and Balwant Singh for pre-production assistance.